The State and the Politics of Development in Nigeria

Adonis & Abbey Publishers Ltd

24 Old Queen Street,
London SW1H 9HP
United Kingdom
Website: http://www.adonis-abbey.com
E-mail Address: editor@adonis-abbey.com

Website: http://www.adonis-abbey.com
E-mail Address: editor@adonis-abbey.com

Nigeria:
No. 39 Jimmy Carter Street,
Suites C4 – C6 J-Plus Plaza
Asokoro, Abuja, Nigeria
Tel: +234 (0) 7058078841/08052035034

British Library Cataloguing-in-Publication Data
A catalogue record for this book is available from the British Library

ISBN: 9781913976156

The State and the Politics of Development in Nigeria

Amaechi Anakwue

ADONIS & ABBEY
PUBLISHERS LTD

Table of Contents

Preface

At a policy discussion during the public presentation of my first book, *Politics of Economic Regulation in Nigeria*, one of the discussants, Professor Sam Egwu, challenged me to do another work on the dynamics and trajectory of the evolution of the Nigerian state as it was raised in part in the book.

I took an immediate decision to embark on this venture. I decided to seek conceptual clarification of the twin notion of the Nigerian state and development or under-development, inquiring into how the variables have shaped the society.

I was concerned and alarmed by the level of under-development in the country, especially as the country remains at the bottom of most global socio-economic indicators, such as poverty rate, child and maternal mortality rate, terror index, illiteracy rate, doctor to patient ratio, open defecation, out-of-school children, and life expectancy.

This is coupled with a parlous economy, as exemplified by the huge debt burden, declining revenue and high cost of governance, and the very weak electoral and democratic systems threatening all state institutions.

There is every need to reverse this trend. The best way to start is to seek theoretical and conceptual operationalization of development, how those in government conceive it, and determine if public spending, projects, policies, and programmes really address Nigeria's developmental problems. The second step is to establish and explain the evolution, character, nature, nuances and dynamics of the ruling class in Nigeria and relate how these bear on Nigeria's development. The last component is to recommend strategies on how Nigeria can achieve genuine development.

The book comprises seven chapters. Chapter one examines the adoption of projects development as a development strategy in Nigeria. The trend continues in chapters two and three, where policies and programmes as development strategies are reviewed. Chapter four is a conceptual analysis of development, chapter five a critique of Nigeria's economic development strategies, chapter six an analysis of the dynamics and evolution of the Nigerian state and its role in the country's development. The last chapter comprehensively reviews the medium- and long-term economic development plans developed and implemented by successive Nigerian governments.

Acknowledgement

This work would not have been a success without the contribution, support and encouragement of many. My mother, Elizabeth Okafor, and my siblings, Ngozi, Amaka, Ifeyinwa, Nkemdili, Omunu and Uju, have remained pillars now and always. It is quite sad that the patriarch of our family, late Chief Richard Anakwue Okafor, is not alive to share in this glory. May his soul continue to rest in perfect peace.

I remain eternally grateful and full of appreciation to the founder, High Chief Raymond Dopkesi, board, management, and staff of DAAR Communications PLC for the opportunity provided me to influence the society in no small measure and contribute my quota towards national development in the course of my work as a broadcast journalist.

Great thanks and appreciation go to Professors Assisi Asobie, Kabir Mato, Abubakar Suleiman, and Ali Zoaka. My unreserved appreciation also goes to Ariyo Olamide, Osaretin Iyare, Jacob Abang, Funmi Emopkae, Sunday Ani, Chidi Nwaokpatu, Godknows Ben, Okey Ugwu, Philip Unugor, Sunday Ani, Habibat Olawoyin Modupeola, Edmund Onwuliri and Ebuka Ogbodo. Gratitude also goes to officials of the Health and Human Services Secretariat, as well as Education Secretariat of the Ministry of Federal Capital Territory, Abuja, especially Mallam Kabiru Musa, PRO and Abdulrazak Laremoh, acting Secretary of Education.

Special appreciation also goes to Sunday Ichedi and Moses Mathew of the National Bureau of Statistics

Dedication

To my Wife, Ifeyinwa, (Osodieme) and my children, Chinonso, Chukwuemeka and Chidike and Great patriots that desire genuine development of Nigeria

Foreword

This book is the author's reaction to the overwhelming evidence of under-development confronting the Nigerian State today. He draws attention to the circumstances and dynamics that brought us to where we are today and submits that we should stop mistaking expenditures by government, fanciful policies, programmes and initiatives for real development. The author deconstructs the presumptions that have guided and which apparently still guides the "developmental" efforts of successive governments in Nigeria by tracing the contradictions we are living with today to the battle for the control of resources by the ruling class.

If, as the author correctly argues, sustainable development continues to elude the Nigerian State because of the failure of successive governments to deploy the right strategies that would properly address the endemic problem of under-development, it must follow that his views on the reasons for the country's current debt profile, shrinking earnings, huge overheads, weak institutions and baffling electoral processes and practices demand more than passing attention. This book compels us to raise the age-old question about the role of such indices as per capita income and GDP in driving genuine development.

The author's further submission that a nation with demoralizing statistics on poverty and which is ranked among the poorest and the worst in literacy, life expectancy, child and maternal mortality rates, terror index, opportunistic criminality, doctor to patient ratio, open defecation, unemployment, inflation rate, out-of-school children and corruption must be on the wrong track, makes a lot of sense. His call for a radical review of the foundations on which successive governments in Nigeria have been trying to build sustainable development for over six decades is, therefore, contextually understandable, if not mandatory.

If all we have to show for the efforts of successive governments over the decades is a now-properly-entrenched practice of using alleged development strategies and programmes as official excuses for the continued plundering of the national till by the political, economic and cultural elite, then it is time to look a little more closely into the affairs, future and fortunes of the Nigerian state. There is an evolving crisis of purpose and identity embedded in all of this. This crisis has become the central marker in a now-generally-shared concern about the trajectory of the Nigerian state in a 21st Century world.

If, as the author correctly submits, what we have consistently considered to be "development projects", new policies intended for growth, programmes and investments designed to improve GDP and per capita income, have not delivered the expected or touted results, then we should stop using them for measuring the welfare of the citizenry. If the confusion, burgeoning poverty, unemployment and reinforced economic and political inequality we see today are traceable to our continued use of the questionable paradigms for measuring development, then it is time to take a second look at everything.

This makes the author's call for a people-centred development framework and strategy, an honest attempt at genuine development. The latter would include the resuscitation of the local economies that actually drive, and affect, the people's well-being and livelihood in real terms. It will also include providing contemporary education, modern health services, political inclusiveness and gender sensitivity.

His recommendations on the way forwarded are best personally read and understood, rather than being pre-empted here.

Dr Amaechi Anakwue deserves commendation for this work, especially for the courage of his perspectives and for his recommendations regarding the economic development plans that could, probably on further review and acceptance, benefit the Nigerian State if implemented by successive governments.

Dr Okey Ikechukwu

CHAPTER ONE

Projects as Development Strategy

D evelopment has, over time, been given different interpretations by people across the world. Nevertheless, it has remained a major area of interest for decades. Schumpeter and Backhaus (2003) argue that economic development poses the second most important problem faced by economists. It is a post-Second World War concept that gained prominence after the six-year conflict. Arndt (1987) posits that the term "economic development" denoting a process that societies undergo was hardly used before World War II. The devastation caused to global economies forced experts, scholars, and governments worldwide to think of the concept as a way to re-build.

During that period, the Bretton Woods institutions—the World Bank and the International Monetary Fund—were established to handle post-Second World War economic devastation. The period was also marked by independence for several African, Latin American, and Asian countries and a global concern for the development of these emerging economies.

Scholars have disagreed sharply on the concept of development. However, there has been some form of convergence since the 1990s on the need to place the people at the centre of development. We shall come to that much later. To many Nigerians, development is erroneously viewed as the speed that physical structures such as buildings, roads, bridges, electricity poles, water supply pipes, and other physical infrastructures spring up. You hear people speak of how development has caught up with a particular locale or community when these physical structures spring up rapidly or when conurbation between two cities, towns, or communities is achieved.

To them, development is all about the physical outlook of their immediate environment. An area is deemed developed if structures are situated there. This layman's concept of development also permeates government circles. The Nigerian local, state and federal governments tailor their activities and public expenditure along this line. This is partly because they do not understand the real meaning, nature, purpose and processes of development. It is also because they see their quest to develop their constituencies as a means to siphon public funds and resources. This erroneous perception of development is deep-rooted, and it will be a herculean task to change this.

It is commonplace to hear political officeholders point to the many structures they built and boast of developing their constituencies. The bulk of public funds are channelled towards constructing these "development projects," ranging from roads, bridges, airports, conference centres, religious centres, stadia, civic centres, recreation centres to public service secretariats, government houses and lodges.

These projects are advertised as "legacy projects" that will outlive political officeholders who will be remembered for many years after leaving office. In many instances, public ratings of political officeholders are tied to these projects.

It has gotten to a frenzy as members of parliament, at the federal and state levels, are now under pressure to be linked to the execution of "legacy projects." As a result, the National Assembly has surreptitiously introduced what is referred to as "intervention projects" into Nigeria's annual budgets. This provision accommodates constituency projects sponsored by every member of the National Assembly.

The lawmakers want to be seen to be involved with these "development projects" as their constituents put them under constant pressure to bring these projects to their doorsteps. They have inadvertently been sucked into the craze for constructing "development projects." They now spend part of their time in supposedly executive functions at the expense of their law-making functions and responsibilities.

According to Olafusi (2019), President Muhammadu Buhari said the government had spent N1 trillion on constituency projects without commensurate impact on the people. Akipelu (2019) also reports that the president made this allegation on the strength of findings by the Independent Corrupt Practices and Other Related Offences Commission (ICPC) that Nigerian federal lawmakers, in connivance with executive agencies, have perfected fraudulent means of pocketing billions of naira under the guise of constituency projects. The anti-corruption agency reached this conclusion after tracking 424 projects from 2015 to 2018.

The ICPC's report noted the weaknesses in ministries, departments, and agencies using its System Study: Ethics and Compliance Scorecard. These weaknesses are even more apparent in the states of the federation.

High-level corrupt practices take place during the procurement and implementation of projects in Nigeria. For example, more than 85 percent of the 378 ongoing corruption cases instituted by the ICPC as of July 2020 are linked to project execution. This is further testimony that projects in Nigeria remain a conduit pipe to siphon public funds.

Can political office holders be blamed for equating development with projects? They have been led to this conclusion because the conversation about development in the country has largely been about "development projects" as the fastest means of achieving economic development. This erroneous belief is perhaps a holdover from colonial times and a derivative of the nature of economic development plans in Nigeria. Nigeria's colonial masters carted away resources from Nigeria under the guise of commodity trade by concentrating on building infrastructure that will aid the production and export of the raw materials. The political class that inherited power from them has been using it for personal aggrandisement.

From the pre-independence Ten-year Plan of Development and Welfare for Nigeria (1946-1956) to the successive development plans up to contemporary times, up till the Economic Recovery and Growth Plan (ERPG) (2017-2020), the underlying idea and philosophy have been rapid development projects, policies, and programmes as the path to national development.

The different economic development plans and blueprints mostly contained a list of projects to be constructed, policies and programmes to be implemented, and the time frame and cost implications. They were short on the philosophy and strategy of achieving real economic development and the place of the citizenry. It was mostly about expenditure on projects, similar to what Labour party politicians in the United Kingdom referred to as a "tax and spend government".

The very first development plan in Nigerian history, the Ten-year Plan of Development and Welfare for Nigeria (1946-1956), had a total planned expenditure of N110 million. The plan did not run its full course. As a consequence of this, a five-year development plan (1955-1960) was launched (Olaniyi, 1998). This plan, like its predecessor, was more of an expenditure plan than a productive one. It allocated 38 percent of total expenditure to transportation, 7.2 percent to education, 5.7 percent to primary production, 5.3 percent to electricity, and 5.6 percent to irrigation.

Following it were the national development plans that also concentrated more on project execution. According to Okigbo (1993), the first National Development Plan (1962-1968) had a total proposed investment expenditure of N2.132 billion, divided into public sector investment of N1.352 billion and N780 million from the private sector.

It was during this period the federal government successfully executed projects like the oil refinery in Port Harcourt, the paper mill in Jebba, the sugar mill, and the Niger Dam (in Jebba and Bacita, respectively), the Niger Bridge in Onitsha and Asaba, ports' extension in Lagos, , and several trunk 'A' roads across the country.

The First National Development Plan was supposed to be national in both composition and implementation. Okigbo (1993), however, opines that it lacked the basic qualities to make it truly national. He asserts that the plan was just a conglomeration of a catalogue of projects each region wished to execute. This pattern of project construction continued with the Second National Development Plan (1970-1974). The political crisis that ravaged Nigeria during the first national development plan and its implications threw up the need for another plan. The need for reconstruction after the civil war and the need to accommodate the new 12-state structure created by the Yakubu Gowon administration made a new plan inevitable.

Launched immediately after the civil war, the second national development plan was designed as a post-war development plan. According to Olaniyi (1998), the plan's philosophy was influenced by the exigencies of the war. Its focus was the reconstruction of a war-battered economy and promoting economic and social development in a country emerging from a civil war. The trend continued with the Third National Development Plan (1975-1980). The plan anticipated an initial investment fund of N30 billion. Ayinla (1998) asserts that the plan carried over the objectives of the second national development plan.

Next was the Fourth National Development Plan (1981-1985), which was considerably bigger than its predecessors, with a projected capital expenditure of N82 billion. The public sector was to contribute N70.5 billion, while the private sector was to contribute N11.7 billion. Again, it followed the pattern of excessive focus on project execution.

From every indication, development plans in Nigeria have largely been project-programme-, and policy -centric. This situation has thrown up and created a development perception founded on a fallacious argument. It has become a tool for the politicization of poverty in the country. Rather than alleviate poverty, create jobs, educate the people, and ensure good healthcare, the projects, programmes, and policies impoverish the people.

Ake (1981) points out that the development strategies and plans of African countries are more often than not an aggregation of projects and policies that may sometimes be incompatible. This lack of clarity indicates African aspirations are not likely to be realised.

Nnoli (1993) avers that development has come to a dead-end in Nigeria partly because of the increasing disconnect between the leadership and the people. The former incorrectly assume that development is possible without the commitment, fervour, and support of the latter. He opines that the people are the foundation of development.

Many "development projects" end up abandoned or uncompleted because the original intention behind their conceptualization and execution is far from real development purpose. Instead, the underlying intention is usually to use the projects as conduits to siphon public funds. This corrupt practice precipitates why many contracts are allegedly inflated and shoddily executed. For example, former Senate President Ahmed Lawan stated that the cost of building infrastructure projects in Nigeria remains one of the highest in the world (Nasir, 2019). This is very strange and may well indicate the level of corruption inherent in the country's procurement process.

Ayobami (2012) reports that 11,886 federal government projects were abandoned in the last 40 years nationwide. This is contained in a report submitted by the abandoned projects audit commission President Goodluck Jonathan set up in 2011 to ascertain the state of federal government-owned projects in the country.

According to Osemenan (1987), Nigeria has become the "world's junk-yard of abandoned projects worth millions of naira." There is a competition by the three tiers and levels of government on projects construction. This was confirmed by Dr Victoria Okoronkwo, the chairperson of the governing council of the Nigerian Chartered Institute of Project Management of Nigeria (CIPMN). She disclosed that the cost of abandoned projects in Nigeria stood at N12 trillion (Adejumoh, Enimola & Asabor, 2019). Some persons, however, believe the figure is much higher. What a drain on the lean resources of a country still grappling with developmental challenges? If the real agenda behind the institution of these projects was development, how then do we explain why many of them are abandoned?

The Nigerian government is not yet done with building projects as plans are on to build more. It launched a national integrated infrastructure master plan in 2015 to address the huge infrastructural gap in all sectors of the economy. It is a 30-year roadmap for infrastructural development that it hopes will guarantee sustainable economic growth. It projects that Nigeria needs $2 trillion to execute this plan. This plan is premised on the assumption that Nigeria's weak infrastructure base is a constraint to its socio-economic development.

The federal executive council approved the plan on November 21, 2012, with the National Planning Commission assigned the responsibility of coordinating its development. Its highlights include a capital allocation framework for 30 years (2014-2043), infrastructure investments spread across the six geo-political zones of Nigeria, an increase in Nigeria's core infrastructure stock as a percentage of GDP from 35-40 to 70 by 2043, identify investment required to bridge the existing infrastructure gap, increase spending on infrastructure from the current 3-5 percent of GDP to an average of 9 percent over the 30-year period, and ensure 2 percent of the GDP is spent on infrastructure maintenance.

This, again, underscores the emphasis on projects as a means of development; pushing valuable funds into projects that have limited bearing on the welfare of the people. This trend may likely continue into the foreseeable future, except the country embarks on radical and fundamental changes in its approach to development.

Let us consider how many of these infrastructure projects have helped alleviate poverty in the country. Going by Nigeria's poverty and inequality rate in 2019 by the National Bureau of Statistics, the states with the highest poverty rate have some level of infrastructure considered "necessary for economic development."

In the report, Sokoto state has the highest poverty rate at 87.73 percent. It is followed by Taraba state with 87.72 percent and Jigawa state with 87.02 percent. Ebonyi and Adamawa states follow with poverty rates of 79.76 percent and 75.41 percent, respectively. See Appendix 1.

As of January 2021, four of the five most poverty-stricken states have airports, with Ebonyi state currently constructing one. In addition, three of the five have multi-billion naira stadia, with Sokoto, Adamawa, and Ebonyi states building multi-billion naira stadia as of February 2021.

So, the most poverty-stricken states in Nigeria have spent billions of naira of taxpayers' money on airport and stadium projects that have not eased poverty. Rather, they may have contributed to the current poverty situation considering the opportunity cost of the funds. This is in addition to many other huge projects that may not have positively impacted poverty alleviation, job creation, and closure of the inequality gaps in the states.

The Jigawa state government spent N11.5 billion to build an international airport in Dutse, the state capital (Okunbor, 2014). What value, in terms of revenue, job creation, ensuring an egalitarian society, and poverty reduction has the airport added to Jigawa state? The airport is clearly not viable and it lacks the necessary facilities to function optimally. On completion of the edifice, the state government entered into an agreement with an airline that operated twice-weekly flights, bringing in between five and fifteen passengers per flight (Okunbor, 2014). The state government subsidizes the cost of the flight operation.

Jigawa state, with over 87 percent of its people living below the poverty line, spent over N11 billion to construct an airport that is unviable and requires huge subsidies to operate. Where then lies the priorities of the government? To build huge airports or empower its people by creating jobs, investing in their education and health, and lifting them out of poverty?

The Nigerian government spends on projects that have had no positive impact on the welfare of the people. Take the Moshood Abiola Stadium in Abuja as an illustration. It was built between 2000 and 2003 at the cost of N54 billion ($360 million) to host the 2003 All Africa Games. Stadiumdb.com described it as one of the most expensive in the world. With a 60,000-capacity, it is a modern stadium city with the facilities to host several sporting events.

The complex has remained in ruins since Games ended in 2003, hosting very limited sporting events and rarely is it filled to capacity.

The dilapidated state of the Abuja stadium as at August 4, 2019 (Picture taken from *The Daily Independent*)

It is a common sight to see newly built roads across Nigeria being used to dry food stuff. The villagers use this method because the traffic count on the roads is quite low. This indicates that the roads are valued as platforms to process farm produce, as many of them are not car owners.

Does it then suggest that the funds used to construct these roads would have been better utilised constructing food-processing plants? Would this have impacted the local economy much more than the road has?

The picture below is a road in Amechi Idodo in Nkanu East Local Government Area of Enugu state. It shows foodstuff being sun-dried along a tarred road, a common sight across all parts of Nigeria where rural dwellers convert tarred roads to food driers.

The National Directorate of Employment (NDE) is the government agency saddled with designing and implementing programmes to combat mass unemployment. It has four major areas of intervention towards mass job creation: vocational skills development, entrepreneurial development, agricultural skills training, and public works programmes. One of the programmes that run under one of these categories is the enterprise creation fund. Under this scheme, loans are disbursed to beneficiaries after rigorous appraisal to ensure the projects to be embarked on are viable. Each beneficiary gets N250,000 to start a business. With that amount, small and medium enterprises (SMEs) can be created. Within the first year, the enterprise might create between two to three jobs. Let us break it down further. The N54 billion spent on building of the Moshood Abiola Stadium would conveniently create 216,000 SMEs and close to 648,000 jobs in a year.

One can also apply the same method in calculating the number of jobs the monies spent on stadia and airports in the poverty-stricken states would have generated if they were utilized for that purpose.

CHAPTER TWO

Policies as Development Strategy

D uring the implementation of the National Rolling Plans (1990-1998), there was a shift in Nigeria's development planning from a project-based system to a policy-based one. Policies such as deregulation, privatization, and liberalization were implemented. That was a remarkable and fundamental shift, and perhaps the biggest since the indigenization policy of 1974.

According to Nnoli (1993), the military ruler that introduced the rolling plans, Ibrahim Babagida, argued that the new direction was informed by the need for Nigeria to exigently make adjustments to its economic policies if it ever hopes to cope with the dynamic economic environment of the 1990s. It came in the form of introducing an economic emergency programme, the Structural Adjustment Programme (SAP), to solve some of the obvious problems plaguing the economy. It also emphasized a private sector-led economy, instead of the public sector-dominated economy of previous development plans. This, however, did not put an end to the focus on projects as many of them were pursued.

The move towards a policy-based economic development strategy led to the introduction of policies prescribed by the Bretton Woods institutions, such as privatisation, commercialisation, liberalisation, and deregulation. We will explain this in greater detail in subsequent chapters.

The other economic development plans, such as national economic empowerment and development strategy, vision 2020, the seven-point agenda, the transformation agenda, and economic recovery and growth plan, described as reformist and transformational, continued the emphasis on projects with the large sums that would go into it. In addition, the policymakers emphasized socio-economic and macro indicators with targets set by the different development plans, including GDP and its growth rate, per capita income, and inflation rate.

One of the critical policy frameworks of Vision 2020 is the expansion of investments in critical infrastructure. It laid out encouragement of private investments as a means of achieving this. Emphasis will be on building on the framework for infrastructure concession where private sector organizations will be allowed to build, maintain, rehabilitate, operate, transfer or own public infrastructure.

In the first implementation phase of the Vision, aggregate investment projections was put at N32 trillion. The federal government was expected to contribute N10 trillion, the state governments N9 trillion, and the private sector N13 trillion.

The intrusion of policies into Nigeria's economic development philosophy came with its negative effects. It created an environment of economic distribution and an allocation model driven by patronage. The opening up of the economy for the private sector to become the engine of growth led to a situation where granting licences, permits, waivers, and approvals to private concerns in various sectors such as petroleum, financial services, telecommunications, electricity, and broadcasting became the order of the day. It also came with granting private concerns privileges to ensure they play their new role in the economy, placing the interest of the private sector over and above those of the people, and paying lip service to the economic interest of the Nigerian people. It is packaged to promote, protect, and advance the private sector's interest by ensuring that it tightens its control of the economy and gives the class exclusive access to Nigeria's resources.

The awards were not based on competitive or objective criteria. They largely went to friends, relatives, associates, and cronies. The resultant effect was inefficiency, corruption, nepotism, and mediocrity. The expected energy and drive from the private sector fell short of expectations. Coupled with a project-driven public sector with abandoned and white elephant projects that make little to no contribution to the economy and welfare of the people, the strain on the economy has started to take its toll.

Uzoigwe (2007) argues that many developing economies opened up their trade regimes under the guise of liberalization are prevented from reaping the benefits because of market-access barriers imposed by developed nations. Moreover, these are labour intensive sectors where developing countries typically have a comparative advantage.

These policies gave the private sector control of the economy, envisaging it will accelerate the country's growth. The government's role is hugely scaled down and concessions are given to the private sector to build critical infrastructures such as power and transport through public-private partnerships (PPP) that gave the whole process legal standing. The PPP could be in the form of build, operate and transfer (BOT) or build, operate, and own (BOO). Under this arrangement, private sector firms are responsible for providing critical infrastructure and running public utilities. They are expected to finance the projects and recoup their investment and make profits by collecting tolls on the infrastructures or fees for services rendered.

This is another way to further appropriate the country's resources and impoverish the people. The private sector is motivated solely by profit, so the tolls and fees to be charged for providing essential infrastructures and services will be exploitative. The legal framework for this exploitation was laid out with the establishment of the Infrastructure Concession and Regulatory Commission (ICRC), which is is expected to regulate the concession of public utilities and services to private firms.

The public-private sector partnership in Nigeria is not conducive to an effective implementation of the policies to achieve its objectives of injecting huge funds into the provision of utilities, services, and infrastructure. One case serves as a good example of this: the concession of the Lagos-Ibadan expressway. The road, the oldest and most busy dual carriage highway in Nigeria, was transferred to Bi-Courtney in a concession. The company was supposed to rehabilitate, expand, it and modernise the road while recouping its investment and profit through tolls. However, several years after the concession was signed and activated, the road remains a work in progress. Usigbe (2012) reports that the federal government was forced to cancel the concession agreement in the face of Bi-Courtney's non-performance.

The same firm also won a concession contract from the Nigerian government to build, operate, and transfer a new domestic terminal at the Murtala Mohammed Airport, Lagos. Though the terminal is up and running, the firm has been in a running battle with the government over alleged violation of certain clauses in the concession agreement.

Continued and full-scale operation of the concession idea will further enable private interests to continue to milk the citizenry, and ensure the further collapse of infrastructure and public amenities. For instance, Williams (2011) reports that the Ministry of Aviation had running battles with Bi-Courtney over allegations of unilateral and unfair hikes in passenger service fees, sometimes by as much as 150 percent.

The choice of the firm for concession contracts is not in any way driven by merit. It is entirely based on patronage. Bi-Courtney, the firm that benefited from the two main concession deals in Nigeria, had a legal adviser to late President Umaru Yar'Adua, Wale Babalakin, as its chairman.

Ahmed (2012) posits that the PPP arrangement cannot work in Nigeria, except a strong regulatory and governance environment is evolved to enable things to be done fairly, competitively, and in the overall interest of the nation. Ahmed also recognizes the near helplessness of the ICRC to effectively discharge its duties due to these limitations. He highlights the weakness of the act establishing the Commission and avers that it must be amended for the Commission to function efficiently. For instance, he pointed out that the Commission can only persuade, and not compel other government agencies, departments, and ministries to protect the public interest when making concession agreements.

The ability of the ICRC to protect the public interest in concession agreements is further weakened by the powers the act establishing it confers on the president: the president can issue general policy guidelines to the commission. Since Nigerian presidents are notorious for favouring parochial interests in their official capacity, it is certain their associates will always have an advantage in the competition for concession agreements.

Touching on the exploitative nature of concession arrangements, Igbuzor (2009) argues that it will put unmerited money into the pockets of the comprador bourgeoisie and impoverish the masses. According to him, when you concession a road, tolls will be collected. The upper and middle class can usually afford these toll charges, but the lower class cannot. As a result, their meagre income will be further depleted, forcing them deeper into poverty. This, he argues, is irrespective of whether the concession has improved the quality of service available. To Igbuzor, this exploitative tendency is made worse in a country such as Nigeria where a good number of the people live below the poverty line.

Members of the comprador bourgeoisie class in Nigeria, their agents, and sympathisers have always put up the fallacious argument that the global trend now is that the private sector is at the forefront of most countries' economies. This is a misleading argument tailored to deceive the masses.

The truth is that countries are now emphasizing using 'the capable state' as the main lever for the development of national economies. This is not without prejudice as some limited level of cooperation with the private sector is essential for the development agenda.

In 2007, the United Nations Development Programme (UNDP)-sponsored 7th African governance forum in Ouagadougou, Burkina Faso came out with a report that describes capable states as prerequisites for development on the continent. A team of experts that attended the forum agreed that countries on the continent should turn their attention to governments with the capacity to meet citizens' needs.

Their argument is hinged on the philosophy that national development programmes should not be based on externally developed blueprints, but should reflect local priorities, aspirations, and designs. In this regard, the government's capacity to finance development interventions should be strengthened to avoid reliance on foreign assistance.

In light of this movement, the UNDP in 2010 started a process of redirecting its aid and grant to African countries to areas that have to do with building a capable and inclusive state. Therefore, the body reaffirmed its commitment to strengthening credible national institutions like parliaments, human rights organizations, and anti-corruption commissions in developing countries. Close to $25 million was thus redirected based on this direction.

Taking a cue from this initiative, Rwanda, when putting its Vision 2020 together, made the institution of good governance and a capable state the main pillar of realizing the vision. The vision document was of the view that the state's role, which is indispensable for wealth creation and development, is presently low in Rwanda and needs to be strengthened.

This is in contrast to the Nigerian economic development plans and policies, which are centred on the private sector playing a lead role in the development of the country's economy, thereby conferring undue advantages to them.

As was argued earlier, for any development strategy or programme to have any meaningful effect and be successful, it must be people-centred. The people must own it, and they must be fully involved with its implementation. Unfortunately, Nigerian development plans and policies do not have this attribute. On the contrary, their focus is on the comprador bourgeoisie. From its formulation to implementation, it is completely alien to the people.

No concerted attempt is made to sell the idea to the people or for them to own it. This is unlike the Rwandan Vision 2020, where the government adopted a very ingenious means of selling the vision to the people by raising it to the level of national discourse. The country, like Nigeria, observes the last Saturday of every month as a special environmental sanitation day. The government takes advantage of this to hold town hall meetings after the sanitation exercise where the vision takes centre stage. According to Habineza (2013), the meetings provide the citizens with an opportunity to evaluate the vision's implementation level and and the performance of those driving it. They get to own the vision in the process.

The different economic development plans and strategies in Nigeria erroneously assume that the people will key into their implementation without a deliberate effort to co-opt them. The policymakers think that the formulation and implementation of the vision involve just a few privileged members of society.

They have consistently argued that there was widespread consultation of experts during the formulation process and a wide spectrum of stakeholders and interest groups were involved in the visioning process. They also argue that since those involved were carefully selected to represent all interests of society, it can be deemed that everybody was carried along.

The process is not inclusive. Igbuzor (2009) argues that development is not just about expert opinion, but the mobilization of the people's aspirations and potential. He is convinced that the consultations are not wide enough. If they were, the formulators would have realized that many Nigerians would want an economic development strategy that would targets improvement in their welfare and create jobs for the unemployed.

Thirty percent of our respondents in the questionnaire we distributed as part of this work suggested a strategy that will focus more on improving their standard of living, while 23 percent went for one that will generate massive jobs. Another 18 percent preferred a strategy that will be agrarian and grassroot-based. Twenty-one percent opted to stick with the vision document as produced by the government.

However, formulators of the Vision 20:2020 were focused on a narrow and selfish objective. Part of their agenda was to create more poverty, inequality, and deprivation among the Nigerian lower class. This situation will engender and sustain the political strangulation and domination of the lower class by the comprador bourgeoisie. If the masses continue to strive for just daily sustenance, the time to think about politics and their political rights will simply not be there. They will ever remain willing to get hand-outs from politicians during elections in exchange for voting for particular candidates.

Husseni (2012) believes that as the vision increases poverty, inequality and unemployment, crisis, such as the type that is ravaging Northern Nigeria, will engulf the country. He also opines that the attendant insecurity and violence may threaten the corporate existence of Nigeria.

It is based on this conclusion that Obadan (2013) averred that the objectives of the vision cannot be realized due to constraints like poverty and poor implementation of agricultural and manufacturing policies. He opines that the relatively strong growth recorded by Nigeria has not translated into the broad-based economic and social development needed to reduce inequality and lift millions of people out of poverty. Instead, the growth recorded has been alongside increasing poverty levels.

The African Development Bank (AfDB) rates the poverty reduction strategies of the Nigerian government very low. In its yearly report, contained in its African economic outlook, the proportion of Nigerians living below the poverty line increased from 65.5 percent in 1966 to 69.0 percent in 2010. On social protection, the report said that though it was a priority in the Vision 20:2020 plan, there is still no comprehensive policy and budgetary support.

The introduction of policies as an economic development strategy in Nigeria ensured the relegation of the state's role in the economic process and the impoverishment of the masses. The more the policies are enunciated and implemented, the more poverty, inequality, and unemployment rise. There is a strong link between the variables.

Most of these policies are at the behest of the World Bank, the International Monetary Fund (IMF), the Paris Club and others. The policies rarely ave a local flavour, and have established the private sector as the engine of economic growth in the country. They have facilitated the dominance of the private sector through privatization, deregulation, commercialization, concession, and public-private partnerships.

There is virtually no aspect of Nigeria's national life that does not have a policy that guides it and provides the wider template for action. Many of them are not even known to the operators and players in these different aspects. It appears their relevance ends immediately after approval by the Federal Executive Council. Ijie (2018) opines that there are inconsistencies in development policy formulation and implementation among the different organs and levels of government in Nigeria.

CHAPTER THREE

Programmes as Development Strategy

Successive Nigerian governments have relied heavily on programmes, most of them ad-hoc, as a strategy for the country's development. Many of these programmes fizzle out as soon as the government goes out of office. They are interventionist in nature, backed by the belief that critical interventions are needed to catalyze the country's development. Most of them target job creation, economic empowerment, and support with the poor and vulnerable, including women, children, and farmers, as the expected beneficiaries.

In 1972, the Yakubu Gowon administration set up the National Accelerated Food Production Programme (NAFPP) and the Nigerian Agricultural and Cooperative Bank (NACB) to ensure adequate funding of agricultural production in the country. The various river basin development authorities and integrated rural agricultural development projects were also established during the period.

In 1976, the Olusegun Obasanjo administration set up Operation Feed the Nation (OFN), which was geared towards encouraging food production and security in the country.

In 1980 the Shehu Shagari administration came up with the Green Revolution Programme, which was aimed at providing more food for Nigerians by reducing the importation of food and increasing crop and fibre production.

In 1989, the Ibrahim Babangida administration established the People's Bank to offer soft loans to the masses to start businesses. The same administration also established the Directorate of Foods, Roads and Rural infrastructure (DFRRI) in 198x. Like the name suggests, it is geared towards providing basic infrastructure to the people in the rural areas to reduce rural-urban migration. It also sought to improve the quality of life in rural areas

In 1986, the administration established the National Directorate of Employment (NDE). The NDE began operations in 1987 and was mandated to curb unemployment resulting from the devaluation of the naira, and the privatization and commercialization of the economy. The same administration also set up the Mass Mobilization for Self Reliance, Social Justice and Economic Recovery (MAMSER) in 1987, which flowed from the recommendations of the political bureau and was tasked with the orientation of the people to enunciate the abstract ideas in economic policy and promote value orientation. It was renamed the National Orientation Agency (NOA) and is in operation up to this day.

In 2009, the Umar Yar'adua administration instituted the Presidential Amnesty Programme (PAP) to end the disruptive protests in the oil-producing Niger Delta. It provided militants a state pardon, educational training, and a monthly stipend in exchange for the surrender of their weapons. The militants were also expected to stop the kidnappings of oil workers and the destruction of oil facilities.

In 20xx, the Goodluck Jonathan administration instituted the Subsidy Reinvestment and Empowerment Programme (SURE-P). The scheme was established to re-invest the federal government's savings from fuel subsidy removal on critical infrastructure projects and social safety net programmes. The hope was that it would have a direct impact on citizens. Its core objective was to provide employment for unemployed graduates through internship programmes, create a database of unemployed youth, and reduce social vulnerability as a result of increased fuel prices owing to removal of petrol subsidy.

In 20xx, the Muhammadu Buhari administration instituted a National Social Investment Programme (N-SIP) to cater to the country's poorest and provide a social safety net for those without employment. The programme was to ensure a more equitable distribution of resources to the vulnerable; the children, youth, and women. One of its major components is the N-power programme, which was set to address youth unemployment by providing a structure for large-scale and relevant work skills acquisition and development while linking its outcomes to fixing inadequate public services and stimulating the larger economy.

Other components of the N-SIP are the Government Enterprise and Empowerment Programme (GEEP), the Conditional Cash Transfer programme (CCT), and the Home-grown School Feeding programme (HGSF).

The Buhari administration also came up with another poverty alleviation strategy, the National Poverty Reduction with Growth Strategy (NPRGS). It was the brainchild of its economic advisory team, the Presidential Economic Advisory Council (PEAC). The NPRGS was established to support President Buhari's audacious pledge to lift 100 million Nigerians out of poverty within a decade. It is anchored on four pillars:

- Macroeconomic stabilization policies to improve the capacity of the economy to absorb shocks and avoid disruptive adjustments;
- Industrialization for economic growth and economic transformation from a commodity-dependent growth path to a diversified, industrialized, knowledge-intensive, and job-creating economy;
- Structural policies and institutional reforms to engender efficiency in service delivery, promote transparency and accountability in the management of fiscal resources, bridge the infrastructure gap, annd improve private sector development and mainstream gender;
- Redistributive policies and programmes to reduce levels of risks, vulnerability, shocks, and deprivation. The latter include programmes aimed at enhancing income, job opportunities, and wealth creation through vocational skills, training, micro-credit and macro-enterprise development, and livelihood diversification in the agricultural sector.

The strategy assumes a gradual annual GDP growth from 2.3 percent to 4.4 percent from 2019 to 2024, and 6 percent per annum from 2025 to 2030. During the period, annual average reduction in poverty is projected to be around 11.2 million per annum, 80 percent of which will be in wage-paying jobs. Redistributive and transfer programmes that target the ultra-poor include vocational skills, MSMEs support, and livelihood diversification programmes. The education and skills embedded in these programmes are expected to provide the entry routes for the extremely poor into the mainstream economy by 2023. In addition, the poverty gap between the south and the north is expected to narrow, as access to education, health, and qualitative standard of living is ramped up nationally and in the north in particular.

Current public sector financial resources are inadequate to fund the poverty alleviation programme on the required scale it seeks to create. Over the ten-year period for which the strategy is expected to be implemented, the total cost for the implementation is an estimated $1.6 trillion. That is an annual average of about $161 billion. A major drawback of this ambition is that in 2020, the total consolidated national budgetary resources for Nigeria, that is the federal and state governments, was approximately $54 billion. The proposed solution is the creation of the an independent corporate institution, the Nigeria

Investment and Growth Fund, with contributions sourced from the local and international private sector. A national steering committee chaired by the vice president shall be the overarching body for anchoring collaborative efforts across federal ministries, departments and agencies, state and local governments, development partners, civil society organisations, and private sector actors.

Many of the economic development programmes have failed to achieve most of their objectives, instead engendering poverty and corrupt practices (Obikeze, Ananti, & Onyekwelu, 2015). They point to the National Accelerated Food Production Programme, the Nigerian Agricultural and Cooperative Bank, Operation Feed the Nation, the Green Resolution Programme,and insist they only produced overnight elite farmers who had no business farming. They opine that the programmes were used by serving and retired army officers, senior civil servants, businessmen, and politicians to acquire parcels of land and certificate of occupancy in the guise of wanting to establish farms. They also believe that some of the programmes were established to compensate political associates who have in one way or the other helped them to win an election.

Abdu (2012) referred to it as the politicization of poverty. He asserts that governments in Nigeria use poverty alleviation programmes to drive citizens into poverty. He argues that the programmes end up making the people worse off than they were before the advent of the programmes.

Okoye and Onyeukwu (2007) highlighted the level of corruption inherent in economic development programmes in Nigeria. They manifest as diversion of resources, and conversion of public funds to private uses.

Why do successive governments create ad-hoc committee to implement economic development programmes? Why do they shy away from using existing bureaucratic structures? Why do these programmes fizzle out as soon as the government that created them leaves office? Answers to these questions point in one direction. Many of these programmes were implemented by hurriedly arranged frameworks. Successive governments were angered by existing bureaucratic and institutional mechanisms designed to execute and implement such development programmes. They preferred ad-hoc and emergency frameworks that usually operated in a taskforce-like manner. What is the attraction for this? Are the ad-hoc arrangements conduit pipes to siphon public funds? Those appointed to supervisory roles and to oversee their implementation are usually politicians who end up hijacking what could have been a crucial interventionist development programme.

CHAPTER FOUR

The Concept of Development

We stated at the beginning that development has, over time, been given different interpretations by people across the world. Even scholars have disagreed sharply on what the concept means. However, there has been some form of convergence since the 1990s on the need to place the people at the centre of development.

Before we go into what we consider the nature, character, and definition of development, let us explore the thoughts of scholars on the concept.

According to Seers (1969), development means and occurs when there is a steady decline in the level of poverty, unemployment, and inequality in a society. The development will likely improve the standard of living of individuals. He further argues that true development lies in the elimination of poverty, increase in literacy, and improvement in the health system instead of the increase of per capita output. Seers also argues that the focus on national income as a target for achieving poverty reduction ignores the real problems of development. He offers policy recommendations to incorporate more socially relevant measures to better address development problems, focusing on education, population growth, and political independence.

He also insists that there is no real development when the benefits of technology and progress help only a small number of people in the developed world, who are already relatively rich. Therefore, he postulates that for countries to develop their economies, they need to maintain strong and inclusive growth, guarantee better access to social services, target policy interventions that protect the poor and vulnerable groups, create jobs, and emphasize wealth creation. He sees a strong causal relationship between his three leading indicators of development: unemployment, poverty, and inequality. Development in any of them implies, helps bring about, or may even be a necessary condition for development in one or more of the others. To reduce unemployment is to remove one of the main causes of poverty.

Todaro and Smith (1969) see development as a multi-dimensional process involving major changes in social structures, popular attitudes, and national institutions, the acceleration of economic growth, the reduction of inequality, and the eradication of absolute poverty. Development, in its essence, they argue, must represent the whole gamut of change by which an entire social system, tuned to the diverse basic needs and desires of individuals and social groups within that system, moves away from a condition of life widely perceived as unsatisfactory and towards a situation or condition of life regarded as materially and spiritually 'better. They also believe there are three core values of development: life-sustenance, self-esteem, and freedom to choose.

Todaro and Smith also suggest that the most accurate method of measuring economic development is the human development index, which takes into account literacy rate and life expectancy, which, in turn, have outright impact on productivity and can lead to economic growth. They took a policy-oriented approach, presenting economic theory in the context of critical policy debates and country-specific case studies to explain how theory relates to the problems and prospects of developing countries.

They explained the unprecedented progress made in many parts of the developing world, and fully confront the enormous problems and challenges that remain to be addressed in the years ahead. They also showed the wide diversity across the developing world, and the differing positions in the global economy held by developing countries.

The field of economic development is versatile and has much to contribute to these differing scenarios. Thus, the authors also underlined common features exhibited by a majority of developing nations using the insights from the study of economic development. The few countries that have essentially completed the transformation from developing to developed economies, such as South Korea, were examined as potential models for other developing countries to follow.

Taking a holistic African perspective, Ake (1981) looked at the dynamics of class formation and contradictions in socio-economic formations, especially as it relates to strategies for the continent's development. He underscored the high desire on the part of African leaders to achieve the development of their countries. This led to the concept becoming an obsession and the leaders elevating development to the point of ideology in the absence of the latter. Ake traced this development to initiatives by the western world, with the United Nations as a key tool in redefining relationships between the erstwhile colonial territories and metropolitan countries. The category "developed" and "underdeveloped" countries were employed as a means of classification.

The African leaders pursued development to be like the West. Ake therefore concludes that most development strategies in Africa were inadvertently tailored by the West.

Using Lesotho as an example, Ake argues that African development strategies lack unique experiences of local history and originality. The objectives of Lesotho's development plan for the period 1974-1980 are to increase GDP, encourage new investments, especially private ones, and diversify of sources of finance. This, Ake opines, fostered the continuation of capitalist development, the confusion of development with economic growth, and indifference to the causes of economic backwardness.

He postulates that what obtains as strategies for development in most African countries are a mere fusion of projects and policies. There is no distinguishable strategy of and for development. This factor leads to ineffectiveness in achieving desired objectives. Why are genuine strategies of development elusive to many African countries? Ake asks. He also provides the answers. It boils down to a few factors. The first is, as he rightly opined, there is the tendency for African leaders to focus solely on policies and goals. They erroneously believe that under-development will be naturally wiped out once there are set goals, policies, and projects.

A second aspect of the problem, according to Ake, is an offshoot of the first. There is the tendency to focus on one or two problems in vogue, such as indigenization, and allow the elaboration of the character of a development strategy. The third reason is the assumption that goals that appear individually desirable are also collectively compactible.

The implication is that the development strategies adopted by most African countries are not clearly spelt out nor systematically pursued. They include expansion and diversification of agricultural export commodities, import substitution, export promotion, integrated rural development, and a basic needs approach.

According to Ake (1981), political conditions in Africa are the greatest impediments to development. Ake dismissed the traditional reasons advanced by scholars as being behind the failure of development in the continent. These include colonial legacy, social pluralism, corruption, poor planning, and lack of entrepreneurial skills. He described them as irrelevant.

He argues that development has not been the primary agenda of the ruling class in Africa since independence. Looking at post-colonial Africa, Ake posits that the character of the state it inherited from the colonial era has remained the same. The competition for political power and its attendant economic rewards by the different social classes and groups ensure that the real developments of African societies are never the priorities of its governments since independence.

The intensive competition has given rise to a situation where the winner uses state power for material acquisition, clamping down on, and preventing members of another class, or of the same class, from acquiring any form of state power. Consequently, politics becomes a zero-sum game, and power is sought and maintained by all means.

Ake posits that the attention of the group or class in power is so concentrated on this struggle that development is completely ignored. And, to further keep the people distracted from the class struggle for power, they introduce the concept of development and development strategies as a smokescreen. In real terms, it gets limited attention and serves hardly any purpose as a framework for economic transformation. What actually passes for development plans and policies are mere aggregations of projects and objectives that mean little for the welfare of the masses; they reduce development to economic growth.

As an alternative, Ake asserts that Africa needs an economic development strategy based on traditional agriculture and political development based on decentralization of power, not one that concentrates power unduly at the centre.

Nnoli (1993) concluded that the economic development process in Nigeria has come to a dead-end as a result of inconsistencies, confusion, and superficiality that characterize the process. He laments the absence of a theory or vision in the management of the Nigerian economy, which has led to the fractionalization of national interests and a general lack of direction in the development process. This, he says, has led to a divide between the leadership and the people, with the upper class erroneously assuming that development is possible without the people. By trying to bypass the people in the development process, Nnoli concludes the process will remain a dead-end.

The upper class, which happens to be in control of the economy and its management, in this confused state of mind go after economic growth in place of development. Their strategy is the achievement of fiscal and external balance in the short term to address the problems of external shocks, unstable foreign exchange, and high interest rates. All these, he argues, are prescriptions of the Structural Adjustment Programme (SAP). They abandon the long-term targets of social and economic transformation that will benefit the lower class. The upper class also ignores the qualitative changes in the society induced by parameters such as GDP, balance of payment, exchange rate, money supply, interest rate, investment rate, and privatisation.

Nnoli also argues against the introduction of privatisation as a solution to the under-utilization of resources for the development of the Nigerian state. Successive governments, he asserts, are of the view, though without proof, that the private sector is more efficient and productive than the public sector. They, therefore, transfer resources, through privatisation, from the public sector to the private sector. The leaders of the private sector, according to Nnoli, have nothing to offer Nigeria in relation to the the development of its economy. They are willing to become millionaires without creating a technological and industrial base.

Nnoli also argues that since 1985, the various governments have imposed a centrist capitalist ideology and politics on Nigeria, organizing an economy and society that produces 'money bags' that are unable to win and exert influence in the society. Economic policymaking by these governments lack theory and are superficial. They are based on mere common sense, dealing with the symptoms of economic problems instead of tackling the disease.

Explaining the reason why the economy is parlous, Nnoli avers that participation is confined to the comprador bourgeoisie, a set of people that are not oriented to production, but to distribution and who objectively are not patriotic due to their dual interest in the nation and the foreign bourgeoisie with whom they are linked by business. This process halts the possibility of a production-oriented and patriotic national bourgeoisie.

In finding solutions to the economic problems of Nigeria, the comprador bourgeoisie resort to mere empiricism, operating from hand to mouth in the manner of firefighting organizations. In pursuing development, there is no attempt to link the phenomenon in the rural and urban areas. Development is viewed in terms of replicating the attractive infrastructures in urban areas. There is no plan for the social and economic transformation of urban areas.

Apart from basing development plans on deep-rooted theory, Nnoli postulates that it must recognize the centrality of the people in the process. The people have a right to determine policies in their interests and control their production process. For any development plan to be effective, it must have a social welfare programme. National wealth must be distributed based on work done. Free education, healthcare services, childcare, and adequate pension and social security insurance must be part of it.

Nnoli anchored his conclusions on the absence of discernable theories and plans for the development of the Nigerian economy between 1979 and 1989. Apart from the SAP, Nnoli asserts that economic management by successive governments has been based on the rule of thumb and a fire-fighting approach.

Chapra (1992) made recourse to the religion to explain why the classical and regular economic development models have been failing and how religious doctrines can remedy the situation.

He asserts that traditional economic development strategies were based on the pro-western premise that religion and morality are not relevant to economic development. In a critique of these strategies, Chapra posits that capitalism is anchored on unfettered private enterprise, profit motive, and the market mechanism. While acknowledging that capitalism led to the expansion of the global economy, it has, however, been unable to eradicate poverty from the face of the earth. On the contrary, wealth and income inequalities have increased, leading to a situation where poverty co-habit with affluence among peoples of the same society. He argues that while capitalism introduced wealth, it did not achieve equity in wealth distribution.

Chapra also extended criticism to socialism. He agrees with proponents of the philosophy on the need to end the exploitation of the masses by a privileged few. However, he disagrees with the belief that those who will organize and implement the redistribution will do so on an equitable basis. He insists that the same motivations that precipitated the exploitation will also push politburo members to corner juicy wealth and property for themselves, thereby defeating the original goal.

On the economic development strategy of the welfare state, Chapra was not convinced that greater roles for the state in improving the functioning of the market and social insurance for its citizens are enough to guarantee equity. This is even with strong government regulation of key sectors of the economy. He further postulates that the forces that create and perpetuate poverty and inequality are too strong to be overcome merely through such ad hoc measures as pushed forward by the welfare state proponents. A thorough reform of the socio-economic structure and values of life will help solve bigger social problems, Chapra opines.

His point of departure is the total absence of equity in economic development plans and strategies. He argues that it only receives lip service such as in India in 1952 and Pakistan in 1956.

Drawing largely from the Islamic world view and economic strategy, one that provides all the elements necessary for human well-being in accordance with the demands of brotherhood and socio-economic justice, Chapra argues that development can only be achieved if adequate attention is paid to reallocation and redistribution of wealth and resources in the society.

For Islamic countries whose economies are still in infancy, Chapra strongly recommends that they adopt whole scale, his ideas, as it will not be difficult for them to adapt to a new design and direction. The strategy subscribes to the Islamic principles of equality of all humans, one brotherhood, collective ownership of societal resources, just acquisition of resources, and equitable distribution of resources. The strategy is to eliminate the price system as the major determinant of demand and supply. The responsibility, according to Chapra, should be left to an equitable system that cares for all and is implemented by the state based on Sharia values.

Sen (1999) argues that freedoms constitute not only the means but the ends in development. She believes that development must be judged by its impact on people, not only by changes in their income but more generally in terms of their choices, capabilities, and freedoms. We should be concerned about the distribution of these improvements, not just the simple average for a society. She also argues that there is no direct link between measures such as a country's GNP growth rate and the real freedoms that its citizens enjoy.

She sees freedom as being central to development and the achievement of development depends on the free agency of the people. For the people to be agents of their own development requires advancement in five distinct types of freedom: political freedom, economic facilities, social opportunities, transparency guarantees, and protective security.

From the foregoing, we can deduce some constant variables are similar, and are like recurring decimals in the conceptualization of development by various scholars. They include access to education, health, employment, freedoms, equality, egalitarianism, decentralization of power, and inclusivity. In attempting our own conceptualization of development, we will bring consider all these factors.

We see development as the tendency of an individual, household, firm and country to provide most of their essential and basic needs within an egalitarian and inclusive society. The basic needs here are good education, good health care, and gainful employment. In other words, these economic units' ability to exist near independently, but in cooperation with others. Added to these is the presence of an egalitarian order that promotes inclusivity in the economic and political order of a society.

The presence of good education, a quality health care system, and employment for most people will inevitably throw up a seemingly egalitarian inclusive order. This is because people that are well educated, have access to quality healthcare, and are gainfully employed will most likely create a society that enthrones such order.

Good education raises the awareness level of a people. It also increases their capacity to know and fight for their rights. It places them on a footing to dissect government policies and programmes, discern the good from the bad, and take steps to reject, resist, and correct abnormalities. Quality education is a plus for a society desirous of progress. The citizens are easy to mobilize by benevolent regimes and national resources are easily harnessed for national development.

A quality healthcare system enthrones a healthy population. Little time is wasted on a sick population and most of the workforce is mobilized for economic activities as the full energy of the people is geared towards increasing productivity. A healthy individual leads to greater income and increased productivity. With good education and a quality healthcare system, an individual would spend less income on these vital areas and, in the process, free up more funds to meet other life needs. This means that an economically engaged person can afford luxuries if the state provides good education and quality health care system. According to the Nigeria Employment Policy (2017), the availability of decent work creates the incentives for individuals to apply their human resources to the fullest to alleviate poverty.

The extent that these economic units conveniently handle these basic needs in a near self-sufficient manner determines their level of development. A position nearer to the self-sufficiency level is deemed as developed and one that is closer to the base is deemed as developing.

This applies similarly to individuals, households, firms, and countries. For an individual, the propensity to rely on oneself to meet these existential conditions determines the level of development. A person educated above basic education level with access to affordable health care and gainful employment is highly placed to handle problems and attend to the basic needs of his environment. If an individual has access to all these, it then means that they can exist and meet the very crucial needs of life. There are other luxuries that fall outside of this category. They are, however, not basic and directly tied to the critical life support of the individual. In other words, the person can easily do without them. One can afford to do without holidays, expensive vehicles and clothing, and mansions. Basic earnings are enough, in the presence of the necessary factors, to guarantee the basics of life.

The same argument applies to households as a collective. The sum of individual earnings and level of exposure to good education and quality healthcare delivery determine level of development. The ability of the household to do this in a near independent manner or reliance on outside help determines how developed it is.

This also applies to firms and countries. In reality, no individual or country is self-sufficient in meeting their basic needs. Sometimes, they depend on outside sources. However, some individuals and countries have attained very high appreciable levels.

CHAPTER FIVE

Critique of Nigeria's Economic Development Programmes

All economic development plans in Nigeria have the same pitfall: undue focus on projects, policies, and programmes that have little or no effect on the masses. This is why the country is at the bottom of the majority of global socio-economic indices.

The sad commentary about this is that the country is yet to realise this huge mistake. The proposed Vision 2050, the long-term economic development blueprint that the Muhammadu Buhari administration is envisioning, has adopted the same strategies, principles, and philosophy of previous blueprints.

If successive blueprints had survived the litmus test or were good enough to achieve their objectives of ensuring the country's development, why is Nigeria on the verge of state failure? The truth is the plans and blueprints were colossal failures whose only gains are some projects that litter the country; projects that trillions of naira are being wasted on to maintain without commensurate impact on the economy and people. These projects end up draining scarce resources that should have goneto improving the welfare of the people.

For example, let us consider the 2018 United Nations Development Programme (UNDP) human development index (HDI). The HDI is a summary measure for assessing long-term progress in three basic dimensions of human development: a long and healthy life, access to knowledge, and a decent standard of living. A long and healthy life is measured by life expectancy; knowledge level is measured by mean years of schooling among the adult population, which is the average number of years of schooling received in a lifetime by people aged 25 years and older; and access to learning and knowledge is measured by expected years of schooling for children of school-entry age, which is the total number of years of schooling a child of school-entry age can expect to receive if prevailing patterns of age-specific enrolment rates stay the same throughout the child's life.

Nigeria's HDI value for 2018 is 0.534, ranked 158 out of 189 countries and territories. This is, from all indications, not just poor but also awful. It indicates that Nigeria, once the reference point for rapid economic development in the Third World, is sinking deeper into poverty and a fragile state.

Table 5:1 Summary of Nigeria's HDI Performance Relative to Selected Countries

	Quality of health (3 indicators)			Quality of education (7 indicators)			Quality of standard of living (4 indicators)			Overall (14 indicators)			Missing indicators
	Top third	Middle third	Bottom third	Top third	Middle third	Bottom third	Top third	Middle third	Bottom third	Top third	Middle third	Bottom third	
	Number of indicators												
Nigeria	0	0	2	0	0	1	0	0	4	0	0	7	7
Congo (Democratic Republic of the)	0	0	2	0	1	1	0	0	4	0	1	7	6
Ethiopia	0	1	2	0	1	0	0	0	4	0	2	6	6

Source: UNDP Human Development Report 2019

We argued earlier that for development to take place, governments at all levels in Nigeria must focus more on critical areas that bear so much on the real development status of the people: education and health. Therefore, the bulk public spending should go towards these key areas. Unfortunately, the reverse has been the case in Nigeria. The country has failed to meet the World Health Organisation (WHO) and United Nations Educational and Cultural Organization (UNESCO) prescriptions on health and education funding. This has transferred the burden and responsibility on the citizenry, in the process eating up a very good portion of their earnings.

When citizens spend so much on these critical areas, it reduces their disposable income and prevents them from spending on other areas that would improve the quality of their lives.

We conducted a survey of household spending on education, health, housing, extended family, and holidays. The aim was to determine the percentage of income that go to each and which expense consumes the most income. The findings showed that education takes the bulk of income at 32.2 percent. This is followed by housing at 24.4 percent and health at 12 percent. Holidays and pleasure accounted for 11.9 percent, and expenses made on extended family members accounted for 10 percent. This leaves just 9.5 percent of income to handle other needs. The areas that take most are those we have classified as critical to human development. Nigerians are spending so much on them because of the near failure of public services due to neglect and under funding. Nigerians are relying more on private sector-provided services, which it is a huge drain on their income. In other climes, these services are majorly provided by the government in a public service manner. Citizens there save so much by avoiding private and profit-oriented service providers. The graphs below will further elucidate the survey.

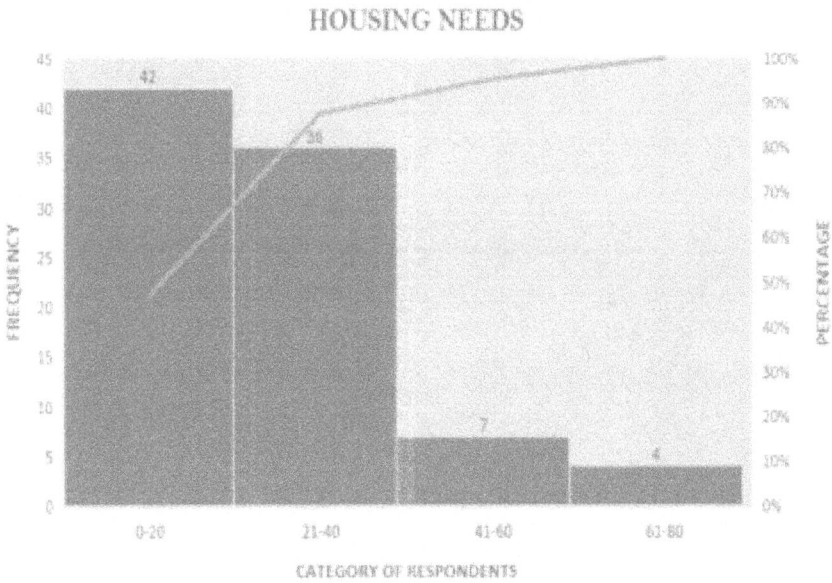

HOUSING NEEDS

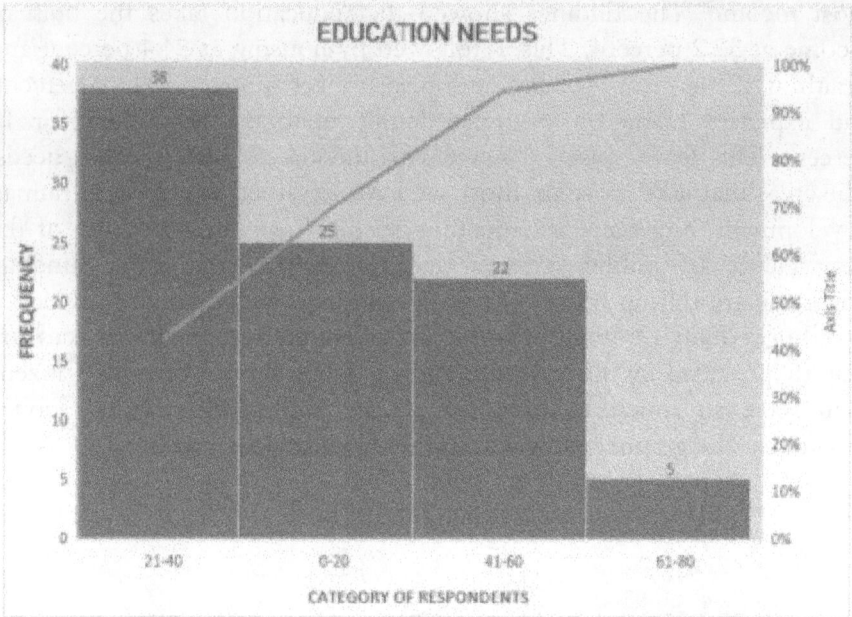

EDUCATION NEEDS

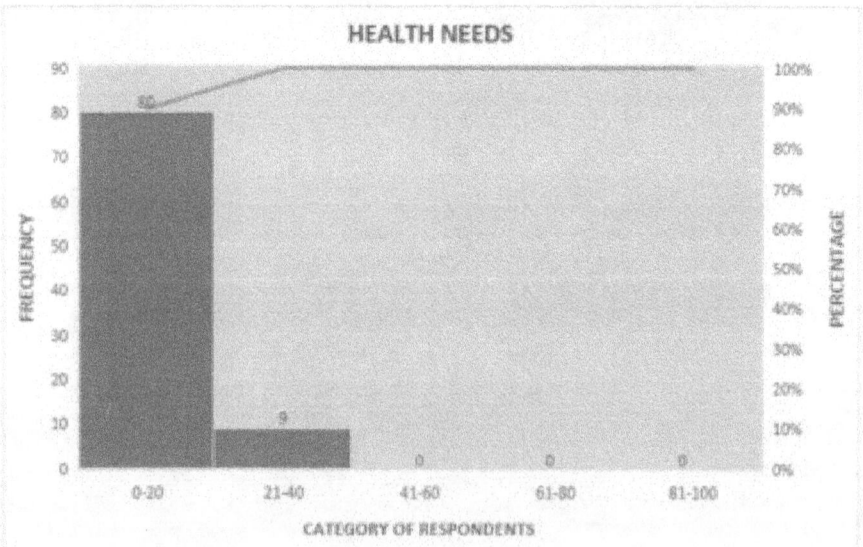

HEALTH NEEDS

EXTENDED FAMILY

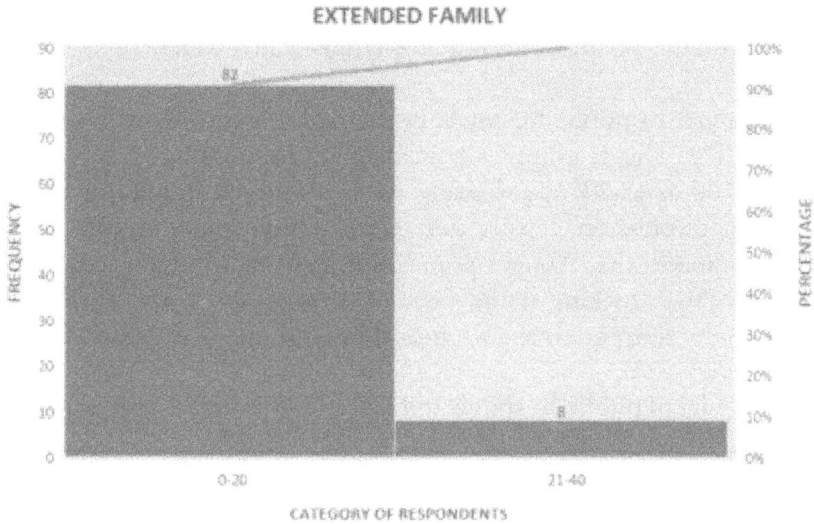

PLEASURE

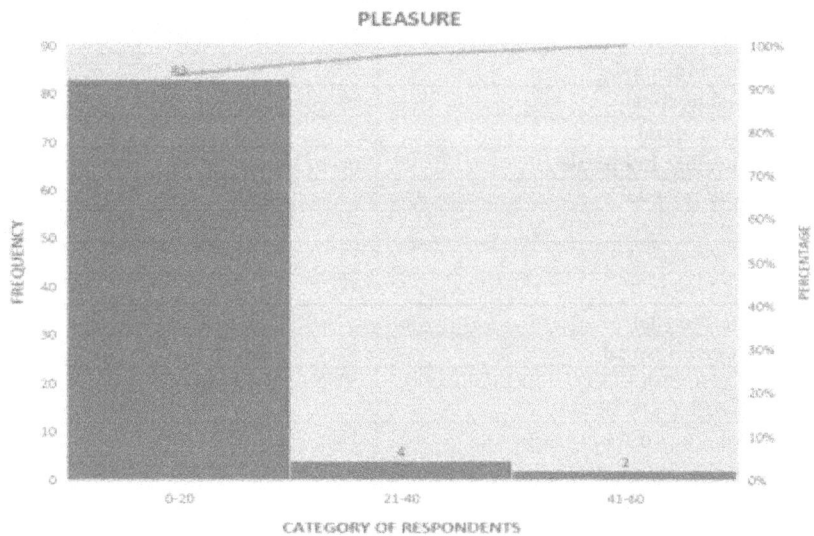

Once public spending on housing, health, and education increases, there will be a corresponding increase in the quality of welfare and life as more money would be freed up for spending on other areas with positive impacts. We also sought from our respondents what areas they would want the government to focus spending on to relieve them of the burden of fending for themselves. Fifty-five percent picked education while 35 percent indicated health care needs. This is a request the federal and state governments must look into and actualize. There are insuffent beds in Nigerian public hospitals, signifying reduced investment in health care delivery.

There are 14 public hospitals in the nation's capital with a total bed space of 972. This is completely inadequate for a city with a population of 3,564,100 as at 2016, according to the National Bureau of Statistics. The 2006 population census put Abuja's population at 776,298. The UNFP estimates that Abuja's population grew by 139.7 percent between 2000 and 2010, making it the fastest-growing city in the world. As of 2015, the city is experiencing an annual growth rate of at least 35 percent.

Table 5:2 List of public hospitals in FCT and number of beds available

NAME OF PUBLIC HOSPITAL IN FCT	NO OF BEDS
maitama district hospital	99
asokoro district hospital	135
wuse district hospital	129
name of suburban hospital	**no of beds**
nyanya general hospital	51
gwarimpa general hospital	99
kubwa general hospital	103
bwari general hospital	60
kuje general hospital	40
name of satellite hospitals	**no of beds**
karshi general hospital	37
abaji general hospital	37
kwali general hospital	55
karu general hospital	37
zuba general hospital	50
rubochi general hospital	40
HOSPITALS OPERATED DIRECTLY BY THE FEDERAL GOVERNMENT	NUMBER OF BEDS
university of abuja teaching hopsital, gwagwalada	360
national hospital, Abuja	500
federal staff hospital	80
Total no of beds	**1,912**

Source: FCT Health Management Board

The hospitals in the FCT were established more than two decades ago, though the Federal Staff Hospital was reconstructed and relocated to a new site with the help of the Chinese government. There is no new public hospital in the fastest-growing city in the world; a clear case of misplacement of priorities by the city's managers. The only new hospitals are privately owned and are drains on the pockets of residents.

You can imagine the stress and pressure made to bear on public health facilities in the city. Most patients, some needing emergency care, are told that there is no bedspace to accommodate them. They either die on the premises of the hospitals, or, for those that can afford them, seek help in private hospitals.

The number of private hospitals and the number of beds in them are far more than public ones. There are 395 registered private hospitals in the city with 3,034 beds.

Table 5:3 Number of private hospitals in FCT and number of beds available

Number of private hospitals in the fct	No of beds
385	3,034

Source: FCT Office of the Registrar, Department of Medical and Diagnostics, Private Health Establishments Registration and Monitoring Committee, Health and Human Services Secretariat, FCT.

The same goes for schools in Abuja as the number of private schools outnumber public schools. According to the Department of Policy, Planning, Research, and Statistics, private schools are much more in number than public schools in four different categories: early child development centres, primary schools, junior secondary schools, and senior secondary schools.

Out of 1,373 schools, 397 are public schools, while 976 are privately owned for early child care development education. For primary schools, out of 1,649 schools, 629 are public schools, while 1,020 are private schools. This trend continues in junior secondary schools where out of 533 schools in Abuja, 364 are privately run, while only 169 are publicly run. For senior secondary schools, there are 186 private schools and 67 public schools operating in the FCT. These figures are for the 2018/2019 academic calendar.

Table 5:4 Number of schools in the FCT: Early Child Care Development Schools

AREA COUNCIL	PUBLIC SCHOOLS	PRIVATE SCHOOLS	TOTAL SCHOOLS
ABAJI	51	21	72
AMAC	129	530	659
BWARI	89	153	242
GWAGWALADA	42	101	143
KUJE	46	115	161
KWALI	40	56	96
TOTAL	**397**	**976**	**1373**

Source: The Department Of Policy Planning, Research & Statistics, FCT Administration

Table 5: 5 Number of schools in the FCT: Primary Schools

AREA COUNCIL	PUBLIC PRIMARY SCHOOLS	PRIVATE PRIMARY SCHOOLS	TOTAL PRIMARY SCHOOLS
ABAJI	16	1	17
AMAC	65	221	286
BWARI	27	66	93
GWAGWALADA	19	35	54
KUJE	25	28	53
KWALI	17	13	30
TOTAL	169	364	533

Source: The Department Of Policy Planning, Research & Statistics, FCT Administratio

Table 5: 6 Number of schools in the FCT: senior secondary Schools

Area council	Public senior secondary schools	Private senior secondary schools	Total senior secondary schools
Abaji	6	2	8
Amac	25	112	137
Bwari	11	33	44
Gwagwalada	10	16	26
Kuje	9	16	25
Kwali	6	7	13
total	67	186	253

Source: The Department Of Policy Planning, Research & Statistics, FCT Administration

It can be deduced that the FCT's priority, which is mirrored nationwide, is not critical areas that will positively impact the people. The increasing private sector investement coupled with the continuing decline in public investment in education is a trend that will continue. That means more misery for the people as they would spend more of their hard-earned money in search of these two critical services. It is too bad and a cause for concern that private-sector spending on education significantly outweighs that of the public sector. Reversing this trend should be a matter of emergency.

Most of the funds accruing to the FCT administration are spent on improving and expanding the infrastructure in the city. The idea is to make Abuja a world-class city comparable to other major cities of the world. The administrators have, however, forgotten the role education and its public funding play in development. In other major world cities, most educational institutions are state-owned.

I spoke with Dr Melitus Abonyi, the chairman, Association of General and Private Medical Practitioners (Abuja chapter), on the hospital investment environment in the city. He highlighted obstacles faced by investors willing to commit their resources to establishing medical institutions in Abuja. They include high operating costs sourcing for buildings, loans, staff recruitment, tough registration processes, high incidence of multiple taxation, and the absence of support infrastructures such as power and water supply. There is a clear absence of support from the government. Dr Abonyi craves a strong will on the part of government to encourage more private sector investments in health care delivery in Abuja.

As the number of abandoned and white elephant projects increase, so also is the bureaucracy. The size of the government has increased tremendously as new agencies are set up, many of which are duplications of the responsibilities of existing agencies. This pushes up the cost of governance and more budgetary allocations to recurrent expenditures than capital expenditures.

These white elephant projects do not positively impact the masses and maybe avenues to loot the treasury. This may explain why, especially at the state government level, humongous projects such as conference centres, ecumenical centres, big government houses and secretariats, and airports are rife. For example, state governments embark on airport projects, which is a capital-intensive project, even when the proximity of existing airports to their states is just tens of kilometres away. The idea is, the bigger the project, the bigger the takeaway.

During these periods, the governments resort to measuring its developmental successes with growth in some socio-economic indicators. They also throw big ceremonies to commission the heavily advertised completed projects, and start to point to the increasing GDP growth rate as evidence that the economy is on the right track.

For the private sector, increases in their balance sheets, profit before and after tax, and dividend pay-outs have become the standard measurement for economic prosperity and development.

Figures from the National Bureau of Statistics indicate that in 2000, Nigeria's real GDP was $69.4 billion. It rose to $176.1 billion in 2005, $363.4 billion in 2010, and $397.3 billion in 2018. This is supposedly an indication that the economy is growing healthily as the size of the economy expands.

Now, let us consider the GDP growth rate. From 5.0 percent in 2000, it leaped to 8.0 percent in 2010 after peaking at 15.3 percent in 2002. It, however, fell to 1.91 percent in 2018 after Nigeria came out of a recession in 2016. The upward movement in real GDP growth in Nigeria and that of the GDP growth rate ordinarily should translate to economic boom, prosperity, and progress for a nation. It also presupposes that the welfare and well-being of the citizens would be enhanced. Unfortunately, in the Nigerian situation, this is not so. As we pointed out earlier, successive governments have relied on these two economic indicators as proof that the economy is steadily improving and that development is being achieved.

Other critical socio-economic indicators that would provide a real and exact picture of how the economy's trajectory has positively impacted the people ignored. Let us consider how unemployment and poverty fared during the same period under consideration. In 2000, Nigeria's unemployment figures stood at 3.9 percent. It increased to 12.3 percent in 2006, 17.5 percent in 2017, and 22.6 percent in 2018. That was after it fell to 5.1 percent in 2010.

In 1996, Nigerians who were classified as relatively poor totaled about 67.1 million. This number increased to 112.4 million in 2010. The National Bureau of Statistics is in the process of updating Nigeria's poverty rate. The poverty rate of Nigeria up to 2010 was based on relative poverty. This means that the rate was calculated using the income level of individuals and households as the basis for determining poverty. Individuals that earn less than $2.00 per day were classified as relatively poor.

However, the method changed in 2020 when the National Bureau of Statistics came out with a more current poverty rate. This time, the Bureau adopted the expenditure method, wherein individuals' spending was the basis for determining poverty level. Those that spent or consumed less than N137, 430 per annum were considered absolutely poor. This spending spans over items in different categories of food, education, housing, clothings and more. Thus, the absolute poverty rate for Nigeria in 2020 was put at 40.1 percent, or 82.9 million poor Nigerians.

From the data above, we can deduce that while the Nigerian economy was growing in terms of real GDP and GDP growth rate, unemployment figures and poverty rate were on the increase during the same period. Thus, while the economy was 'growing,' the majority of citizens were worse off for it.

Successive Nigerian governments have made socio-economic indices such as GDP growth rate and GNP per capita income the end of their development efforts. It is misleading. They are only means to an end. The end remains the welfare and wellbeing of the people. These include poverty alleviation, job creation, and an egalitarian and inclusive society. The socio-economic indices are only means to achieve this end. Where they fail to do so, as we have gleaned from the Nigerian society, we should search for other means. The means may change, but the ends remain constant. With an increase in GDP and other indicators, the hope has been that the wealth being created will trickle down to the people. It has not and may not.

This situation supports our argument that the development strategies employed by successive governments in Nigeria has been defective and ineffectual. Their impact has been superficial and without depth, making no meaningful impact on the life of citizens. Development was far from being achieved despite huge sums of money spent on numerous projects and implementing several policies and programmes. The welfare and wellbeing of the people were not the priorities.

Igbuzor (2009) postulates that Vision 20:2020 is a product of the deceitful Nigerian state. The state, according to him, is now an instrument of deception. Therefore, he argues that the vision cannot develop the Nigerian economy.

In 1990, the United Nations resolved to adopt a system of measuring development by recognising the people as the real wealth of nations. Since then, the development initiatives of the global body have centred on the real needs of the people. Accordingly, they have concentrated on poverty, jobs, education, and the health of the people.

For instance, the UN's Millennium Development Goals had eight goals set towards eradicating global poverty. The goals all bear on poverty alleviation, education and health needs, and equality and inclusivity for the citizens. They are:

- To eradicate extreme poverty and hunger.
- To achieve universal primary education.
- To promote gender equality and empower women.
- To reduce child mortality.
- To improve maternal health.
- To combat HIV/AIDS, malaria, and other diseases.
- To ensure environmental sustainability.
- To develop a global partnership for development.

The same also goes for the Sustainable Development Goals (SDGs). The UN in 2015 outlined 17 life-changing goals to replace the MDGs. Just as with its predecessor, the new development initiative is people-centered. They are:

- No poverty
- Zero hunger
- Good health
- Education
- Gender equality
- Clean water
- Clean energy
- Economic growth
- Industry and infrastructure
- No inequality
- Sustainability
- Responsible consumption
- Climate action
- Life underwater
- Life on land
- Peace and justice
- Partnership

Compare this with the economic development plans of successive Nigerian governments that has been about superficial growth rather than development. Attention has been on growing the economy through GDP and its growth rate, GNP, Foreign investments etc, factors that hardly bear on the welfare and well-being of the people. This philosophy has to change.

Huge sums of money have been spent by different Nigerian governments without commensurate impact on the welfare and wellbeing of the people. These spendings have been channelled to wrong ends with barely any impact on job creation or the poverty status of citizens.

To guard against this, we propose that the government should prioritise poverty alleviation and job creation in its expenditure. The key questions to ask before any project, programme, or policy is announced and implemented are:

1, What will be the impact on job creation?
2, What will be the impact on the poverty status of the majority of the people?
3, How would it impact inequality and inclusiveness?

If this is done, poverty and unemployment would have been mainstreamed into the governance processes. It will factor in the interest of the majority of the people. It is quite sad to state that the projects, policies, and programmes of the Nigerian government at all levels have been pro-elite. They far removed from the masses.

Mainstreaming poverty and job creation would curb this. What do I mean by this? Before any project or programme is executed, the job creation and poverty alleviation impact must be ascertained. Tis can be called the Jobs Impact Assessment Report (JIAR). If the impact is viewed as not commensurate with jobs to be created and how it would impact the welfare and well-being of the local populace, it should be jettisoned. It should be modelled after the Environmental Impact Assessment (EIA) report that promoters of major projects are required to produce before actual construction starts. Legislation to this effect would strengthen the practice.

If answers to the questions are negative, it presupposes that the project, programme, or policy should be jettisoned.

Under the Nigeria Employment Policy (2017), a labour-based intensive public works programmes was enunciated to serve as a major instrument for addressing unemployment. It falls in line with the argument of the International Labour Organization (ILO) (2011) that promoting labour-intensive road construction will generate twice the number of jobs that capital-intensive road construction and irrigation would.

The employment policy aims to use government investment programmes as instruments to generate employment, reduce inequalities, and provide income support for Nigerians. It prescribes that the government shall continuously monitor and assess the employment potential of government investment, procurement, and expenditure in general.

These steps are supposed to become mainstream after the project construction has taken off, but before the commencement of the projects. It should be the main determining factor for the final investment decision (FID) for public projects in Nigeria. Leaving this at the policy level may not fetch the required dividends. It should be legislated with criminal liabilities for public office holders that ignore the provisions of the law.

Nigeria should move away from the use of big machines and plants to execute public works and projects. The labour-inten strategy must replace the machine-intensive strategy. The country should rely more on manual labour than plants and machines whenever it is feasible. This may sound crude, but it will surely guarantee jobs and create wealth by putting money in the pockets of citizens. Of what use are heavy plants and machinery when a better substitute is available.

The country must also rely on technology that is home-grown to execute public works. Reliance on foreign technology does no good. The hope that it will be transferred has never come to reality. It will never. No matter how crude local and indigenous technology may appear and sound, it holds the key to the country's development. It will improve over time since it is the one that the people can readily relate to. This technology exists in abundance but has been neglected over time. Foreign technology is not designed for our local environment. The indigenous ones would create jobs and grow the economy much more than anticipated.

One can imagine how emotionally attached locals would be to, for example, a hospital project in their area if able-bodied men and women were engaged as labourers with the adoption of a labour intensive strategy for its construction. They will practically own the project even long after construction has ended. Memories of money made in the construction will help provide the attachment. A project that community members were consulted during the conception process and are involved in its construction may not need special security for its protection. The community, if they become attached to it, would almost guarantee its safety during and after construction.

Communities who were not involved in both the conception and execution of projects in their area would be alienated from it. They will view it as a government project that only provided an opportunity to loot public funds through a fraudulent procurement process. They will be right in this perception as many of such projects were driven by corrupt considerations.

The current public expenditure system in Nigeria has led to a situation where the country has become the world poverty capital as of 2019. The projects may have exacerbated the poverty situation in the country as smallholder farmers lose their farm lands to these projects, most times without getting due compensation. Without farm lands for subsistence farming, these farmers are pushed deeper into poverty.

Investments and expenditure on education and health bear so much positive impact on the poverty level. That is why the WHO and UNESCO prescribed percentages of national budgets that should go to the two critical areas.

Ensuring that spending of a state's resources is channelled to productive and the above-listed priority areas is key to reducing poverty, creating jobs, reducing inequality, and evolving an inclusive society.

Sodipe and Ogunrinlola (2011) established that the high level of unemployment currently experienced in Nigeria can be attributed, ceteris paribus, to the relatively low employment intensity of GDP growth as measured by the observed employment elasticity of 0.05.

They also discovered that the negative relationship between employment and foreign private investment points to the fact that private investors are using the 'wrong' production technology. That is, using a capital-intensive rather than labour-intensive production method in a labour-surplus economy like Nigeria.

Alternatively, the foreign investors might use FPC to create jobs, but they are not for Nigerians. They are for their own nationals who they bring down to Nigeria to do the job. Several implications for policy formulation and further research can be gleaned from this study. First, given the observed low elasticity of employment relative to the recommended benchmark, the public sector has a key role in job creation alongside the private sector. Thus, in addition to providing the necessary macroeconomic environment for economic growth enhancement, government policies on the quantum and direction of public expenditure are expected to improve job creation, which is expected to increase the level of output. Second, the negative relationship between the log of FPC and EMP is probably an indication that the foreign capital in the Nigerian economy within the period of study is not labour-intensive, but is capital-intensive. An appropriate policy to reverse this trend is expected to contribute significantly to job creation. Third, by mainstreaming job creation in government projects, policies, and programmes, the government will help create and protect jobs.

There has been a culture and practice of foreign firms that execute major projects in Nigeria importing labour from their country. We see Germans and, more recently, Chinese take charge of major road, bridges, and rail projects across the country. They import labour from their country and, in the process, rob Nigerian workers of job opportunities.

In Nigeria, the major indices adopted by government institutions in evaluating economic performance are mostly GDP growth rate, per capita income, and inflation rate. Accordingly, the economic development plans, medium-term plans, annual budgets, and the macro-economic projections of the monetary policy of the Central Bank of Nigeria are focused on the indicators.

Uwaleke (2020) insists that the core indices are missing in this context. Instead, he demands that job creation or losses and the number of people in and out of poverty should become the dominant indices. This argument is very valid. Several countries, including the United States, are more interested in the number of jobs created than in GDP growth rate and size as means of evaluating economic performance. Therefore, reliance on GDP, as is the case in Nigeria, does not explain the economy's real performance.

Dynan (2018) argues that GDP, as currently defined, is not a comprehensive measure of welfare or even economic well-being. He also argued that the exclusion of non-market activities that bear on economic well-being merits more attention, particularly given the potential for such activities over time to change the degree to which changes in GDP capture changes in well-being. Therefore, the reliance on GDP is very misleading and should be considered along with other indicators.

An analysis of sectorial budgetary provisions in Nigeria between 2018 and 2020 reveals the importance the government attaches to key sectors of the economy. The allocations to the most crucial and strategic sectors, education and health are far below expectations. Let us consider the tables below.

Table 5:7 Nigeria's 2018 Budget (N9.12 trillion)

SECTOR	RECURRENT EXPENDITURE (in billion naia)	CAPITAL EXPENDITURE (in billion naira)	TOTAL BUDGETRAY PROVISION (in billion naira)	PERCENTAGE OF BUDGET
Defence	418.8	157.7	157.7	6.3%
Education	439.3	102.9	542	5.9%
Health	269.9	86.4	356.3	3.9%
Agriculture	53.8	149.1	202.9	2.2%

Table 5: 8 Nigeria's 2019 Budget (N8.92 trillion)

SECTOR	RECURRENT EXPENDITURE(in billion naira)	CAPITAL EXPENDITURE (in billion naira)	TOTAL BUDGETRAY PROVISION (in billion naira)	PERCENTAGE OF BUDGET
Defence	418.8	157.7	157.7	6.3%
Education	463.5	47.2	510.7	5.7%
Health	315.7	57.0	372.7	4.1%
Agriculture	57.6	107.2	164.8	1.8%

Table 5:9 Nigeria 2020 Budget (10.59 Trillion Naira)

SECTOR	RECURRENT EXPENDITURE (in billion naira)	CAPITAL EXPENDITURE (in billion naira)	TOTAL BUDGETRAY PROVISION (in billion naira)	PERCENTAGE OF BUDGET
Defence	784.5	116.1	900.6	8.5%
Education	501.4	185.3	686.7	6.5%
Health	538.3	109.5	647.8	4.4%
Agriculture	58.6	124.4	183	11.7%

The allocations to education in the three years was under seven percent, falling short of UNESCO recommendation that countries should allocate between 15 and 20 percent of their budgets to education as contained in a report by UNESCO—Education for All (EFA) (2000-2015): Achievement and Challenges—and the 2015 World Education Forum final report. Beyond the UNESCO recommendation, our stance on prioritising education demands that governments, especially those of developing countries, must devote more funding to the sector. The same applies to the health sector. Going by the three-year Nigeria budget analysis, the allocation to health failed to reach the five percent mark. This is very poor by all standards. The country would not make any meaningful development if this trend continues.

Schultz and Appleby (2019) opine that investments in human capital are critical because they enable children to grow into active citizens as adults. They also believe that targeting investments to maximize human capital can place countries and their populations on equal footing. According to them, that is why international organizations compare the development trajectories of countries based on their aggregated metrics spanning child survival and quality of education available to citizens, especially young people. They also argue that the most consequential investments are those that that enable children to become active citizens as adults.

The federal and state governments in Nigeria are quick to justify limited investments, resources, and expenditure on education and health with the argument that there are other competing areas and needs. They explain that these areas cannot be abandoned to prioritise education and health. This may be far from the truth.

Like several scholars in Nigeria like Prof Claude Ake, we have argued that development is not the priority agenda of the political class in Nigeria. Instead, the primitive accumulation of values has been the driving force of public expenditure and finance. The above argument of areas competing for lean resources does not hold water. The case of universal basic education in Nigeria is further proof that development is not the primary agenda. Under the act establishing the Universal Basic Education Commission, state governments are to provide matching funds before they can access funds to improve basic education due to them from federal resources. All the states of the federation have been unable to access the funds due to their failure to provide the counterpart fund. These funds are lying in waste, waiting for states to do the needful to qualify to access them. As of July 22, 2019, the thirty-six states of the federation and the Federal Capital Territory have N51,612,874,700.70 (fifty-one billion, six hundred and twelve million, eight hundred and seventy-four thousand, seven hundred naira and seventy kobo) waiting to be accessed because they have failed to provide the counterpart funds. They will rather allow the funds lie in fallow than move to access them. This would definitely not be the case if they truly prioritised education. Please, find a state-by-state breakdown of the unassessed UBEC funds below. See Appendix 2.

Civil society and rights activists have been consistent in advocating that chapter two of the 1999 Nigerian constitution be made justiciable. The government of the day should derive motivation from Section 17 (3)d, which states that there should be adequate medical and health facilities for all persons. Section 18 (3) also asks the government to direct its policy towards ensuring free, compulsory, and universal primary education, free secondary education, and free adult literacy education. Many may argue that these are not enforceable, but reason demands that the government approach it as so.

CHAPTER SIX

The Nigerian State and Economic Development Challenges

In determining the Nigerian state's role in the country's economic development, we have to first establish its nature, nuance, and character. To do this, we shall also trace the evolution of states across the world with particular reference to the Nigerian situation.

The modern state has a history that goes back to the state of affairs of Western Europe before the Treaty of Westphalia (Nnoli, 1986). Before then, the basis of the structure of societies was feudalistic. In a bid to exist, co-exist, and reproduce, man had to contend with and engage in different conflicts. This led to the rise and fall of kingdoms (Igali, 2014). The sacred and the temporal were the two hierarchies and parallels that existed in society. The conclusion of the thirty-year war in 1648 led to the Treaty of Westphalia.

Under the treaty, a central bureaucracy within a given territory supported by an army that subsumed spiritual and temporal authorities emerged (Nnoli, 1986). This bureaucracy gave rise to the modern state system in Europe and several parts of the world.

However, the prevailing state system was altered when new dimensions were added with the introduction of the charter of the United Nations and the activities of its agencies. Nnoli (1986) also asserted that developments such as globalisation and the French Revolution of 1789 further altered the state system that evolved from the Treaty of Westphalia.

What then is the state we are referring to? As we stated in previous chapters, the meaning and concept of the state have been as controversial as that of development. However, as Onuoha (1993) observed, despite the analytical difficulties of the concept of the state, it has continued to form the bedrock of political analysis and the science of politics.

Therefore, for the purposes of this book, we have adopted the political economy theory to conceptualise the state.

According to Marx (1848), the state is but the management of the common affairs of the bourgeoisie. He believed the modern bourgeoisie society did not do away with class struggles, but established new classes, new conditions of oppression, and new forms of struggle in place of the old ones. He sees the state as the expression of the class struggle between the two dominant classes in the society: the bourgeoisie and the proletariats. The former comprises owners of means of social production and employees of wage labour, while the latter represents wage labourers who, having no means of production of their own, are reduced to selling their labour to survive.

To Marx, society is shaped by the relations of production, and it is the society that shapes the state. The state is the result of class conflict and provides the means of class reproduction, exploitation, and dominance (Willyard, 2015). Vladimir Lenin sees the state as a form of coercive power, a mechanism of class domination, legitimizing capitalist order and mystifying the masses, allowing capitalists to make decisions behind the scene. The state, therefore, reflects class relations through instrumental control (Willyard, 2015).

According to McLellan (1960), Lenin sees the state as a special organization of force, an organization of violence for the suppression of some class. To Nichos Poulanzas, the state is reflective of the social relations of capitalist class factions. Each state branch or apparatus and each of the respective sections and levels frequently constitute the power base and favoured representatives of a particular faction, instead of certain others (Poulantzas, 1978). Poulantzas' state maintains relative autonomy, meaning it is separate from but tied to the means of production. The state is not an instrument of a unified capitalist class, but representative of capitalist class factions that mobilize to form power blocs.

Goddard et al. (1996, also take Marxist political economy to mean ways in which society's social, economic and political aspects interact. It is concerned with how the state and its associated political processes affect the production and distribution of wealth, and, in particular, how political decisions and interests influence the location of economic activities.

In this process, there is an intensive interaction between two major concepts: state and market. Their two conflicting goals express this interaction: the market seeks to locate economic activities where they are most productive and profitable, while the state, represented by the dominant class, the bourgeoisie, is propelled by the need to capture and control the processes of economic growth and capital accumulation. As a result, the accumulated capital becomes an exclusive preserve of the dominant class as they are guided by principles of territoriality, loyalty, and exclusivity. This inequality in the production process is replicated endlessly in all aspects of societal life; in the distribution of income, the distribution of political power, the allocation of status, and more.

Leslie (1960) provides further insight into how the state and its structures and institutions are employed to advance the interest of the dominant class. He argues that the power generated in the economic sphere, through exploitation, is merely transferred into political power. Political considerations are therefore subordinated to economic ones.

Leslie posits that the powers of the state are generally made to serve the interest of the bourgeoisie. Furthermore, as the struggle for economic resources continues in the society, the dominant class tries to enlist the powers of the state in its support.

Van de Berg (1988) expresses similar views. He asserts that the upper class in every society owns a disproportionate amount of the wealth and contributes a disproportionate number of its members to the controlling institutions and key decision-making groups of the country.

Domhoff (1979) also argues in the same vein. He describes the ruling class as having a disproportionate influence on the political process and effectively dominating the process. As a result, it imposes its policies and programmes on the members of the lower class. He also linked the vast advantages major corporate interests enjoy over the rest of the population to their control of decision-making processes. Domhoff is also of the view that the owners of these corporations and their surrogates dominate, and are over-represented in the executive, legislative, and judiciary branches of the government. This influence is extended to the ivory towers, media, and other critical segments of society. The lower class in society is left at the mercy of the propertied class. They cannot keep up with the competition and struggle for resources.

Miliband (1969) argues that the competition is not on equal terms. He asserts that big businesses enjoy a massive and decisive advantage. The propertied class employs its control and influence to thwart any attempt to change the system, and ensures that reforms are limited to only those that will not threaten its hold on the resources. Miliband places great emphasis on the attitudes, ideologies, and prejudices of elites to explain the behaviour of capitalist states (Umney, 2013). Miliband asserts that the power exerted by business and its allies is not one of various competing influences on the state, but instead is a decisive one. Moreover, far from this dominance being open to challenge by the democratic process, the system is entirely biased in favour of the perpetuation of this power. He believes business and state elites tend demographically to be drawn from the upper class and, consequently, have an interest in maintaining the status quo.

For Ake (1985), the state is essentially a capitalist phenomenon since one of its distinguishing characteristics is a high degree of commodification. He sees the state as a specific modality of power domination, one in which class domination is mediated by commodity exchange, so that the system of institutional mechanism is differentiated from and associated with the ruling class and society. The state, therefore, appears as an objective force standing alongside society. The state thus fails to rise above society and becomes part of its social contradictions because of its role in the production process.

Because the state cannot separate itself from survival, ethnic, religious and other primordial factors, it becomes part of society's problem. The state, therefore, becomes a reflection of the contradictions of the ruling class.

With particular reference to Africa, Ake asserts that the failure to achieve a measure of economic growth is contributing to the development of contradictions and consciousness in socio-economic formations. Members of the capitalist class in Africa engage in very little productive activity. Instead, they derive their wealth through political corruption by using state power for appropriation, which leads to unchecked exploitation (Ake, 1981).

Can one then argue, based on the above definitions and conceptualization of the state that the present Nigerian society fits into any of the variants? To what extent has the state emerged in the country? Is it still in the process of formation? What level of inter- and intra-class contradictions, homogeneity, and coherence are inherent in the Nigerian state or ruling class? What explains and accounts for the instability, disarticulation, and high poverty level within the Nigerian society?

There exists in the Nigerian state a semblance of what Poulanzas (1978) posits: that the state is not an instrument of a unified capitalist class, but representative of capitalist class factions that mobilize to form power blocs. People of diverse economic backgrounds constitute the ruling class in Nigeria. There are feudal lords that have found accommodation within the ruling class. There are those who found themselves within the clique due to their monarchical background. There are also those that have risen to the topmost level of the political structure and bureaucracy, such as public service and political offices, as well as the academia and security institutions. The latest entrants and whose numbers are gradually expanding are the owners the means of production, the nouveau rich that are fast expanding their economic frontiers. The ruling class in Nigeria is centrifugal in nature and operation. Its divergent socio-economic background accounts for this. A new group that controls the cyberspace and information and communications technology is gearing up. This group is populated by leading figures in cyberspace, those that have built up and acquired some economic resources based on their control of ICT. Their emergence is not limited to Nigeria. They have already taken commanding height in advanced nations. These groups of persons are at the top of lists of the richest persons on earth due to their new-found wealth from social media platforms and internet apps.

Extrapolating from Ake's (1981) postulation, the Nigerian state is an objective force standing alongside society. However, the state has failed to rise above society. Because it cannot separate itself from survival, ethnic, religious and other primordial factors, it becomes part of society's problem. The state, therefore, becomes a reflection of the contradictions of the ruling class.

The heterogeneous nature of the Nigerian state is therefore mirrored in the larger society. Each component of the ruling class is based in and draws support from the larger society. This, no doubt, makes the contestations and dialectics untidy and, sometimes, violent.

The loyalty of members of the ruling class and those of the citizens first go to their sub-group and interest before that of the state. As a result, policies, decisions, actions, and inactions, including those at the international level, reflect the sub rather than the overall national interest. Expectedly, this further weakens the country and erodes nation-building.

It is not easy to find Nigerians that are absolutely loyal to the country. The sub-interests are given prominence over national interests as they play the role of pseudo-state and nation for citizens. What are the roles of the state? It provides security and economic opportunities, including jobs and social security.

In Nigeria, the state discharges these functions in the most inefficient means. They have been hijacked to an extent by these sub-interests. How do you expect citizen's to swear allegiance to the state when sub-national interests readily offer services that are the responsibilities of the state?

This is also reflected in local and international programmes and policies of the Nigerian government. They, sometimes, only reflect the interest of sub-groups of the ruling class, especially the ones that enjoy preponderance at a material time.

Bugaje (2018) understands this predicament. The associated result of what he referred to as lack of elite consensus in Nigeria are poverty, unemployment, and instability.

We have continued to emotionalize and trivialize national discourse. We have detained the whole country at some cross road, unable to move in any direction for we don't seem to agree in which direction to pull the country. And as the old line goes, 'no winds are favourable until one knows to which port one is sailing.

Once the elite decide to focus on the future of their country, particularly, security, economy, human capital, infrastructure, the conversation is bound to change. What we need to salvage our country is an elite consensus on where we need our country to be in the next ten/ twenty years, as the first necessary step. We then walk back to assemble the ingredients necessary for the realization of this vision. An elite consensus will free us from distractions and allow us to focus on the most important task of growing our country and will also allow us to marshal all the human and material resources needed to achieve our target (Bugaje, 2018).

One can argue that based on this, the Nigerian state is still in the formation process. There is no specific modality of power relation and domination yet. The domination of all interests by the ascendant interests is needed to achieve cohesion and uniformity in the operations of a state. The level of commodification of the economy and society is still in infancy. The dominance of the interest of sub-groups within the ruling class is still evident. It prevails and transcends those of the emerging capitalist sub-class. Existence, production and reproduction, and subsistence are largely determined by one's position in relation to the dominant sub-classes in Nigeria.

Appointments into various positions in the private and public sector, allocation of values, contract awards, and the general political economy are principally guided and determined by one's relationship with the ruling class. This may well explain why merit, excellence, competence, and capability are relegated in the governance process in Nigeria, which has created room for identity politics and behaviour patterns. It simply pays. Until and when commodification improves and dominates and allocates parochial interests would largely guide values, identity interests, economic and political decisions. Commodification would improve when the emerging capitalist sub-class edge over other interests within the ruling class.

The heterogeneous nature of the ruling class in Nigeria is also reflective in the political composition and configuration of the country. Politics in the country is devoid of ideology, which is not out of place. The existence of ideologies in any society is conditioned on the existence of a class of people that share values or a belief system. It is also premised on a set of attitudes towards the various institutions and processes of the society and ideas that are logically related, ones used to justify the status quo or to change a status quo (Bello, 2008).

As a whole and in blocs, the country's ruling class are yet to effectively put forward an acceptable value or belief system that will serve as a springboard for the country and a standard regime for relations of production. The inter-play of sub-class interests has not given room for the emergence of a dominant class whose ideology will prevail.

If there is no truly dominant interest or class, then the society would not have a subsisting ideology. It would then amount to too high an expectation to expect ideology-driven political parties and processes in the society. The disarticulation within the ruling class in Nigeria reflects in its political processes. It is the same development that shapes its economic processes. Politicians are motivated by one reason; access to state power as a means to primitive accumulation of value.

Even when the manifestoes of the different political parties slightly differ in content, the underlying philosophy is usually jettisoned once political offices are achieved.

Chengdan, (2010) highlights the need for uniformity in a country's ruling class.

A modern country must be unified, because if not unified, it is not possible to mobilize the manpower and material resources of the country to form a unified strength.... In Europe, unification means eradicating feudalism, ending the dominant role of nobility, restricting their influence, and most important of all, depriving them of their ruling power over their own fief. In one word, the political power must be centralized and put into the hands of the central government.

Fadakinte (2013) argues that the Nigerian state is weak, arising from the fragmentation of the dominant class and resulting in a factional struggle for power and chaos. This inhibits the institutionalization of the hegemonic order that should create the guiding values of the society. Thus, because the state is weak and the dominant class is fragmented, a hegemonic process cannot be instituted.

To put it in a simpler frame, governance in Nigeria is an interplay of the interests.

Feudal lords that control large expanses of land are tied to traditional institutions that are very powerful, influential, and play a major role in determining the government of the day at both the federal and state level. Several government policies and programmes are couched to protect, promote, and advance their interests.

Why do politicians always visit the palaces of traditional rulers during electioneering campaigns? Getting their overt or covert support has remained very crucial in swaying voters' support. They remain one of the major routes to getting government appointments; reaching out to an influential traditional ruler will almost certainly guarantee an appointment.

Ditto for religious leaders. They are highly revered and influential. They affect and, to an extent, determine government socio-political and economic policies. They also sway votes and secure appointments and deals for those that are tied to their apron strings.

The top echelon of the bureaucracy, including the security institutions and the academia, are also in this mix, including the retired ones that control enormous wealth and support.

The capitalist and business sub-class, which I consider to be fast emerging, make up sub-class sub-groups that constitute the ruling class in Nigeria. They were in the periphery of the ruling class at independence, but have been steadily gaining ascendancy over the decades. This sub-group holds promises of effecting overall dominance of the ruling class with their present trajectory.

Let us illustrate the dynamics of the Nigerian ruling class with some examples.

Oluwajuyitan (2020) is of the view that feudalism is institutionalised in Nigeria. He asserts that feudalistic interests go a long way in shaping the policies and programmes of the Nigerian government.

Fasan (2020) explains the level of penetration of feudalism in contemporary Nigeria:

> Feudalism? Yes. While the South tends towards progressivism, the North is extremely conservative. Progressivism is based on the idea of human progress, of improving the human condition. But conservatism promotes entrenched privilege, feudalism and a static social order. Going back to the beginning of self-government in Nigeria, Chief Obafemi Awolowo and Dr. Nnamdi Azikiwe pursued progressive policies to liberate the minds of their people and enhance their social progress, but in the North, Alhaji Ahmadu Bello stoutly defended a static social order, where people's social backgrounds were deemed to be destined by God and thus should determine their place in life. Social mobility was not the policy goal that it was in Western and Eastern Nigeria.

The greatest hold feudalists within the ruling class have on the country can be better explained with the status of the Land Use Act in the country's constitution and the entire gamut of the land tenure system.

Before we take a look at the Land Use Act that came into force in 1978, let's dwell a bit on the land tenure system that operated before the law came into effect and introduced a uniform right of occupancy system.

Oshio (1990) states that prior to the introduction of a uniform rights of occupancy system, Nigeria operated a plural system of land tenure. There were basically four systems: tenure under the received English law, tenure under state land laws, tenure under the land tenure law, and the indigenous tenure under customary law. Two of these operated nationwide, while the others followed the usual north-south dichotomy that characterised Nigeria. The power to allocate lands was shared by the political authorities and monarchical feudalists that held sway in the period before and after independence. In some cases in southern Nigeria, it was more communal-based, which further entrenched feudalism.

The 1978 Land Use Act vested all lands in the territory of each state of the federation in the state governor, to be held in trust and administered for the use and benefits of all Nigerians. The Act preserved pre-existing interests in land, subject to their transformation into rights of occupancy. Several Supreme Court decisions have made clarifications of the Act, including the right of communities to hold land.

The move was to protect the long-term economic interest of the country as the existing land tenure system was seen as an impediment to the country's rapid economic development. However, the Land Use Act only entrenched feudalistic hold and control of lands in Nigeria. As Oshio (1990) asserts, monarchs still regard themselves as community trustees for land management and control. They still allocate, partition, and sell land without reference to the state governors. In some instances, what the governors do is legitimize the illegality by integrating the ownership of such lands into the state system with the granting of rights and certificates of occupancy, perhaps out of reverence for the monarchs. This is done through recertification and regularization of such lands.

The Land Use Act has a colonial character. It denies Nigerians' right to own lands, disempowering them in the process. It reduces citizens to the status of squatters and further subjugates citizens to feudal lords. Allocation of lands by state governors and the minister of the Federal Capital Territory is not based on any objective criteria. It is one of patronage where the influential get large expanses of land. It has provided an opportunity for feudal lords to continue with their land grab. Therefore, the majority of the people are turned to peasants whose well-being and sustenance are made more dependent on feudal lords. As Ojo and Offiong (2018) observed, due to the huge capital investment in grabbed lands, local subsistence farmers and pastoralists are now taking an interest in casual paid jobs, which do not pay well.

Efforts to reform the land tenure system in Nigeria and free it from the control of feudal lords have met fierce resistance. Many have called for the Land Use Act to be expunged from the Constitution and turned to an Act of Parliament to make it easy to amend, but this has been rebuffed by the feudal lords and their agents within the ruling class.

The political, bureaucratic, security institutions, academia sub-group of the ruling class are co-landlords within the Nigerian ruling class. They have sustained their hold on this position by using their position in the top echelon of the political structure, security, academic, and public service in the country to amass wealth. Those that rise to the top of these institutions help themselves to the "free money" available. The absence and weakness of institutional mechanisms to ensure probity and accountability in the management of public funds provide the perfect milieu for unbridled and unrestrained looting of the public treasury.

Using their privileged positions, they have systematically frustrated attempts to reform, improve, and strengthen accountability in public expenditure. They are united in this purpose to plunder the resources of the country. One only gets to hear of attempts to expose and punish those who corruptly enrich themselves when there is an unresolved dispute over sharing the loot.

They control the recruitment process into these institutions and ensure elements of the process, such as elections and competitive merit-based procedures, are truncated. They have thus succeeded in capturing state institutions by ensuring that the replacement generation of the headship of these institutions are their cronies. The capture of these critical government institutions cements their place within the country's ruling class and asserts their strong control of the economy, policy formulation, and policy execution. They also are in charge of the legislature, where they dictate the nature of laws to be enacted and amended.

Iwara (2016) argues that state capture in Nigeria is a major cause of the prevailing poverty and underdevelopment. He believes it accentuates the thinking that the capture of the environment and its under-utilization resulted in the mono-cultural economy that hs narrowed the economic space for the people. He concludes that state capture is counter-productive as it undermines the historical and developmental achievements of the country.

By their strategic position in the government, this sub-group of the Nigerian ruling class asserts control over the major means of production and the economy. In response to the need for them to protect their interests, they pay avid attention to the process, content, and direction of economic policies with the ultimate aim of making them align with their class' strategic interest.

Those in this sub-class struggle to maintain their socio-economic status after retirement from public service. By losing easy access to the country's resources, the wealth they accumulated begins to wane right before their eyes. Lacking the ethos to produce and having only the one to consume, they fail to sustain their ill-gotten wealth. It s just a few that successfully retain their wealth with smart investments. A few of them graduate into the next sub-category of the Nigerian ruling class.

The emerging capitalist sub-group in Nigeria's ruling class is perhaps the newest entrant into the privileged top hierarchy in the country. They were not directly involved during the formative stages of the Nigerian society. However, we can provide links between them and the imperial metropolitan bourgeoisie that colonialism paved the way for their intrusion into Nigerian society.

The existence of a sophisticated market system in pre-colonial Nigeria, according to Michael (2015), is the reason ancient Nok terracotta, Benin bronze casts, Kano cloth weaving and dyeing, Awka blacksmiths, and Igbo-Ukwu bronze casts were famous. For these industries to have flourished, Michael argues, the main factors of production—land, labour, capital, and entrepreneurs—must have existed in pre-colonial Nigeria. Anakwue (2019) posits that the dominance of the state in Nigeria's economy during this period does not pre-suppose that the private sector was dormant. On the contrary, they had a good foothold on the economy.

The many private organizations that existed and were active participants in the pre-colonial Nigerian economy—John Holt, United African Company, Peterson Zochonis, Lever Brothers, Leventis—continued to expand in the newly independent state (Ajayi, 1999). They were joined by indigenous companies that operated mostly in the transport, retail, and marketing end of the economy. The ranks of the emerging bourgeoisie in Nigeria was swelled with the implementation of the indigenization policy in 1974. Ogbuagu (1983) states that the policy's objectives were to set the stage for greater participation by Nigerians in the ownership, management, and control of productive enterprises in the country.

Privatisation of publicly owned enterprises by successive Nigerian governments also helped create an opportunity to consolidate the emergent bourgeoisie in the country. The policy was thrust on Nigeria by the Bretton Woods institutions in the 1980s, after the country experienced structural economic imbalance and had to rely on loans to remain afloat. As a result, several public enterprises and utilities were transferred to members of the emergent bourgeoisie under questionable circumstances.

A law—Decree No 25 of 1988—was promulgated to give legal backing to the transfer of national assets to private and foreign businessmen. After the return of democracy in 1999, the Obasanjo administration modified the decree and named it the Privatisation Act.

A technical committee on privatisation and commercialization was created to facilitate the privatisation process. A privatisation council headed by the vice president was also constituted. A total of 111 enterprises were slated for sale, with the Bureau of Public Enterprises (BPE) saddled with the responsibility of fast-tracking the process.

Between 2000 and 2014, 143 enterprises were given out wholly or partially to the private sector, according to documents sourced from the BPE. Out of these, 10 were given out to core investors, 42 went out by way of core investor sale, while another 10 were liquidated. In addition, one enterprise went through the process of guided liquidation, 34 changed hands via concession, with another 12 enterprises also through mineral concession.

A further breakdown shows one enterprise was revalidated for sale, one went by the mode of shares sold to institutional investors on the floor of the Nigeria Stock Exchange, and one by sale to existing shareholders, while nine went by way of share floatation. One enterprise was sold off through public offer of shares at the stock exchange, nine through asset sale, and one through willing buyer/willing seller mode. One other enterprise was sold through core investors willing buyer/willing seller initiative, while eight went off by way of private placement. The remaining two were sold off through private placement and debt equity swap.

A great chunk of Nigeria's wealth was thus handed over to the private sector, in the process giving it a stronger foothold in the Nigerian economy. That perhaps marked a new turn in the public-private sector holdings in the Nigerian economy (Anakwue, 2019).

With this wave of massive privatisation, private capital made some breakthroughs into sectors that were hitherto te exclusive preserve of the state. A classic example is the power sector. The sale of majority equity in the generation and distribution segment of the sector was the biggest privatisation effort in the whole world as the proceeds wer the biggest haul in any privatisation effort globally.

After consolidating their strategic position within the Nigerian society, the emerging bourgeoisie saw another opportunity in the gradual introduction of concession as a policy in the management of the country's vital economic assets.

The Infrastructure Concession Regulatory Commission (ICRC), the agency saddled with coordinating the concession of projects in Nigeria, in December 2016 published a list of 77 projects it hopes to give away.

Under the concession, key infrastructure in roads, railways, ports, and aviation are transferred to private sector control and management at various stages of development. Only two are at the procurement stage, while 75 others are at the development stage as of 2017 (Anakwue, 2019).

It is clear that the strategic hold the emergent bourgeoisie have on the Nigerian ruling class and its grip on the country's economy can only expand in the years and decades to come. They are beginning to have more influence in the politics of the country, through campaign finance. Leading members of the private sector are being named members of critical government committees. They affect and influence public policies and programmes. There is no major economic development plan or policy that they do not have major inputs in. They have floated several organizations that enhance their hold and influence on government and governance. Some of them include the various chambers of commerce and the Nigeria Economic Summit Group (NESG).

Their position will be enhanced with the implementation of effective electoral reforms. With reforms, votes will count, and with enhanced credibility of elections, politicians will be more dependent on campaign funds to mobilize and sway voters. The bulk of these funds will come from the emerging capitalists. That would be after a strong anti-corruption culture has scaled down or prevented government officials from plundering the state's resources, part of which they deploy during elections.

The situation of the emerging bourgeoisie class is aided by the attitude of the Bretton Woods Institutions, which strengthens their hold on the Nigerian economy. According to Kahn (2006), in the past 20 years, donors have advised (and often pushed) governments of developing countries to reduce their direct engagement in the economy – to liberalise their markets, privatise state-owned enterprises and utility companies, and focus the role of the state on policy development, regulation, and the provision of basic services.

Despite this external push, the emergent bourgeoisie has several miles to cover in entrenching their hold on the Nigerian state and economy. Economic governance laws and the prevailing economic, social, and cultural practices need to be retooled to align with a market-dominated and driven economy and society.

For instance, tenancy laws protect tenants, and some argue that they are skewed against landlords. Some of these laws include the Recovery of Premises Act 1990, which is the law regulating landlord and tenant relations in Abuja, the Rent Control and Recovery of Business Premises

Laws of various states in Nigeria, and the Tenancy Law of Lagos

State, 2011.

Isiekwe (2020) is of the view that the effects of these laws being over-protective of Tenants is that it discourages investments in Real Estate and Housing Sector. The subsequent lack of investments in this sector, he also asserts, would mean that fewer homes will be built. There is a huge housing deficit in Nigeria presently and this may worsen.

The dialectical contradictions within the Nigerian ruling class are reflected in the policies, programmes, and laws the country formulates. This is especially so for economic policies, as scrutiny of these policies reveal that they reflect the interests of these sub-groups, especially the one enjoying ascendancy at the material point in time.

Onuoha (2008) argues that two contending social forces—the Nationalists and the Reformists—are currently struggling for the soul of the Nigerian economy. This struggle and the subsequent state capture have perpetuated the economic crises and made revamping and sustaining the economy impossible. He also argues that no progress would be made except the social forces resolve their differences.

Kohli (2012) describes the society Onuoha (2008) envisages as a neo-patrimonial state. According to him:

> Neo-patrimonial states, by contrast, tend to have a weak sense of public purpose, such that ideology does not play a very significant role. Pronouncements of public goals are usually cloaks for the pursuit of personal and sectional interests. The organizational underpinning of neo-patrimonial states also tends to be underdeveloped: much of politics tends to be pre-class, interest groups are often not well organized, and public bureaucracies lack competence and professionalism. Without a coherent ideology and effective organizations, neo-patrimonial states lack developmental power and are rarely capable of defining and pursuing economic goals. Such economic growth as occurs in these settings therefore is likely to occur in spite of an ineffective state, rather than as a result of state action. Economic resources controlled by the state are instead likely to be put to corrupt use and end up in the hands of elites for private consumption, leading to failed efforts at state-led development.

Leaders of fragmented-multiclass states generally preside over states in which power is not highly concentrated, usually not so much because of a deliberate democratic design as because of weak political institutions that encourage intra-elite divisions and limit a state's downward authoritative reach in the society.

These leaders are generally also committed to a broad set of goals, and a variety of interest groups within these states make their demands known to the ruling elite. As noted above, given the competing goals they face, these legitimacy-sensitive elites work closely with business only on some issues and only some of the time. Since political and economic elites may often work at cross-purposes and since the demands of numerous other groups may also require attention, power resources of fragmented-multiclass states are often dissipated and there is an upper limit on how rapidly they can propel industrialization.

This may well explain why successive Nigerian governments tilt towards a neo-liberal economic philosophy or a Keynesian model for their economic policies and programmes. Sometimes, the policies and programmes are guided by market forces, while at some other times, they are influenced by state interventions in the economy. A particular sub-group of the ruling class benefits depending on how the pendulum swings.

The emergent bourgeoisie in Nigeria holds the promise to become the stabilizing factor, at least, going by their ascendancy to control of state structures to stabilize the polity and ensure order. They have the greatest need for order, stability, and due process of the law to be entrenched in Nigeria due to their massive investments in the country. They would be the most affected if anarchy sets in as their investments would be hugely affected by wanton arson and looting. Moreover, businesses thrive in a friendly ad peaceful environment, which is to their advantage. Due to their strong stake in Nigeria's stability, there is a strong probability that they will strengthen their hold on the economy and society's superstructures.

CHAPTER SEVEN

Economic Development Plans in Nigeria

Pre-Independence Development Plans

The history of economic development plans in Nigeria is better appreciated if one goes beyond the country's pre-independence history to unearth the historical and philosophical underpinnings of the whole scope of development plans and strategies.

The description of efforts by the colonial government to institute a development plan will help elucidate those instituted by the successive governments after independence in 1960. A history of such plans will also make room for a better appreciation of the present-day strategy.

The first effort towards development planning in Nigeria by the British colonial masters dates back to 1945. The new Labour government that assumed office in Britain after the Second World War issued instructions to colonial administrations, including Nigeria, to prepare formal plans for their development.

This was informed by the need to ensure the guaranteed flow of natural resources (Okigbo, 1993). Ravaged by the war, Britain urgently needed reconstruction and needed a steady flow of much-needed resources from its colonial territories for this purpose. A development plan in these areas will ensure the colonial economies are strong enough to guarantee its flow.

Thereafter, the Nigerian colonial administration formulated the "ten year plan of development and welfare for Nigeria." According to Ogunjimi (1997), the plan had a total planned expenditure of N110 million for ten years, starting from April 1, 1946, to March 31, 1956.

As Ayo (1988) observes, the plan focused on building a transportation and communications system, while little provision was made for industrial development. The plan was also selective in its focus on agriculture, focusing more on cash crops such as cocoa, cotton, groundnut, and timber. Little attention was paid to developing the productive base and defining a comprehensive development objective for Nigeria.

The colonial development plan was meant to serve the interest of the colonial masters, not that of Nigeria. It was in consonance with the general objective of the British colonial government, which was primarily concerned with the advancement of its economic interest. There were no specific economic targets in the plan. In addition, there were no macro-economic parameters to use as guides since the national income figures and other aggregates were not available.

However, the ten-year plan of development and welfare for Nigeria did not run its full course (Salawu et al., 2012). A series of developments arising from the drastic structural changes taking place in Nigeria due to its development aspirations led to its alteration. The ten-year period was too long to implement a development plan as the swiftness of development in the country rendered some of its provisions ineffective.

A decision was made in 1950 to break the plan into two five-year sub-periods and formulate a new plan for the sub-period 1950-1956. The introduction of a federal system of government through a new constitution affected the revision as each of the regions became autonomous and adopted different economic policies.

According to Olaniyi (1998), the consequence of this was the launch of a five-year development plan for the period 1955-1960. The plan guided the central and regional governments until the first national development plan came into being. It was more of an expenditure plan than a production plan. It allocated 38% of total expenditure to transportation, 7.2% to education, 5.7% to primary production, 5.3% to electricity, and 5.6% to irrigation.

During revisions of the ten-year plan, the World Bank sent a team to Nigeria to help the colonial government in its development efforts. The team made recommendations in a 1954 report that suggested a five-year planning and execution period (Gboyega, 1989). The report also provided insight into the means through which government could raise revenue to stimulate the country's development.

The World Bank's recommendations included setting up several institutional arrangements for easy execution of existing plans and formulation of future ones. Consequently, the national economic council was created in 1955 to provide a common platform where the central and regional governments could address the country's development challenges. The council was also to oversee the planning and coordination of economic policies. It was presided over by the Governor-General with four ministers representing the regions. In 1958, the federal government created a Ministry of Economic Development that served as the secretariat of the National Economic Council (Okigbo, 1993).

In his assessment of the nature of development plans that existed before Nigeria's independence, Okigbo (1993) opines that economic development planning in the pre-independence era had socialist-welfare overtones, but it was not democratic in terms of the participation of the people in either its formulation or discussion of its objectives. He concludes that it followed the British tradition of reserving energy, rail, coal, and main utilities as the preserve of the state.

First National Development Plan (1962-1968)

The attainment of independence in 1960 meant Nigeria had to put a new development plan in place. Besides, the tenure of the last five-year plan formulated by the colonial government expired by 1960. In addition, the need for a truly national plan, one that relates to the country as a whole and has the backing and authority of the national state, was enormous. It came with components for regional governments. Therefore, it was truly national in preparation and content; a partnership between the federal government, regional governments, and the private sector.

The First National Development Plan (1962-1968) aimed to achieve national targets in a specified time by rational use of resources to be mobilized nationally (Qayum, 1975). Its ultimate objective was to harness Nigeria's rich endowments to improve its citizen's living standards. Its targets included ensuring economic growth by at least by 4 percent per annum, achieving self-sustaining growth within the projected future, increasing the country's GDP, thus raising the per-capita consumption by 1 percent, ensuring the growth of the education and health sectors, increasing real income, provision of employment opportunities and better living condition, and attaining a standard economy consistent with the democratic, political, and social aspirations of its citizens.

According to the plan, the priority areas were agriculture, industry, transportation, and human resources. The second set of priorities included social services and infrastructure, while the remaining were classed under the third order of priority.

It was envisaged as the take-off stage for the diversification of the Nigerian economy, to give a sense of direction to the economy, a sense of priorities and urgency, and to enlist the support and cooperation of all sections of the community to work for a better future.

A total investment expenditure of N2.132 billion was proposed. Out of this, a public sector investment of N1.352 billion was expected, while the private sector was to contribute N780 million.

Its objectives and targets as culled from the document were:

- To surpass past growth rate of economy of 3.6 percent per year compound to achieve a rate of 4 percent per annum, if possible to increase this rate.
- To achieve this aim by investing 15 percent of the Gross Domestic Product, and at the same time endeavouring to raise the per capita consumption by about 1 percent per year.
- To achieve self-sustaining growth not later than the end of third or fourth national plans. This involves raising the domestic savings ration from about 9.5 percent of GDP in 1960-61 to about 15 percent or higher by 1975 in order to sustain the bulk of domestic investments.
- To develop as rapidly as possible, opportunities in education, health and employment; and to provide access for all citizens to these opportunities, this includes training of a greatly increased number of doctors, the provision of a greatly increased number of places for university students, the provision of primary education for a rapidly increasing proportion of children of school age, the expansion of hospital services commensurate with the ability of the economy to sustain them.
- To achieve a modernised economy consistent with the democratic, political and social aspirations of the people. This includes the achievement of a more equitable distribution of income both among people and the regions. It includes more specifically:

- the creation of more jobs and opportunities in non-agricultural occupations, -- the provision of advisory and training services to Nigerian businessmen to enable them to compete more effectively at home and abroad,
- the increase in the production of export crops through better seed distribution and more modern methods of cultivation as well as, through the increase in the area under cultivation,
- the introduction of more modern agricultural methods through farm settlements, co-operative plantations, improved farm implements

such as hydraulic hand presses for the expression of palm oil, and a greatly expanded agricultural extension service,
- the expansion of the installed capacity of electricity generation to 643 MW by 1968,
- the expansion of railway mileage by the remaining 293 miles of the Bornu Extension; and an additional 3.6 million tons
- the expansion of a system of a system of tarred roads by about 2000 miles; and completion of new River Niger bridge in Onitsha and second mainland bridge at Lagos, and
- the expansion of cement capacity to not less than 980,000 tons per year

• To maintain a reasonable measure of stability through appropriate fiscal and monetary policies directed to promote the stability of the Nigerian pound and to avoid recourse to physical controls as far as possible.

During the First National Development Plan, the federal government successfully executed projects like the oil refinery in Port Harcourt, the paper mill in Jebba, the sugar mill, and the Niger Dam in Jebba and Bacita, the Niger Bridge in Onitsha, ports' extension in Lagos, and construction of several trunk 'A' roads across the country.

It is interesting to note that it was also during this period that the first-generation universities were established: University of Ibadan and University of Lagos by the federal government, Ahmadu Bello University by the Northern Nigerian government, University of Nigeria Nsukka (UNN) by the Eastern Nigerian government and the University of Ife (now the Obafemi Awolowo University) by the Western Nigerian government.

The First National Development Plan was supposed to be national in both composition and implementation. Okigbo (1993) is, however, of the opinion that it lacked the basic qualities to make it truly national. He asserts that the plan is only a conglomeration of a catalogue of projects that each region of the country wished to execute.

Each region's list was almost like those of others. There was no attempt at the centre to plan the development centrally to enable each region to optimize its material advantages and increase the regions' inter-dependence in a truly national economy. Okigbo opines that had any such attempt come from the centre, it would have been sternly resisted by the very powerful regions (1993). The development plan was more or less made up of four plans: one for each region and one for the central government. The political rivalry between the heads of the regions prevented the possibility of developing a truly national plan.

Another reason Okigbo doubted the national outlook of the plan was that its coverage was limited to only public sector expenditures. It did not specify how the private sector would meet its assigned objectives. Another pitfall of the plan, as articulated by Tekena et al. (1989), was its assumptions that over 50 percent of its funding would come from foreign sources, through grants and aid. The foreign inflow fell way below expected levels. The lack of local skilled labour also took its toll on the implementation of the plan. The foreign experts that helped the National Planning Commission draw up the plan left the country, leaving an inexperienced local staff to spearhead the plan's implementation (Ikeanyibe & Imhanlahmi, 2009).

In 1960, the economic planning unit in the federal ministry of economic development had only two senior staff. By early 1962, there were eight of them, but six had moved elsewhere by 1965. As a result, the unit could not oversee the plan's implementation. The situation was worse in the regions, according to Dean (1966).

Political upheavals also took their toll on the plan. The crisis in the Western region, which culminated in the creation of the Mid-Western region, and the civil war ensured distortions in the plan implementation. The additional component state was not accommodated in the plan, and the civil war saw the diversion of project funds to the war effort.

Second National Development Plan (1970-1974)

The political crisis that ravaged Nigeria during the first national development plan threw up the need for another plan. In addition, the need for reconstruction after the civil war and to accommodate the new 12-state structure created by the Yakubu Gowon administration made a new plan inevitable.

Launched immediately after the civil war, the second national development plan was designed as a post-war development plan. Its focus was the reconstruction of a war battered-economy and the promotion of economic and social development in a country emerging from a civil war. However, a dictatorial military government carried out the formulation and implementation of the second national development plan. It can therefore not be said that it enjoyed widespread consultation and participation.

According to Olaniyi (1998), the plan's philosophy was influenced by the exigencies of the war. This includes building a united, strong, and self-reliant Nigeria, a great and dynamic economy, and an egalitarian society. Attempts were made to rectify some of the shortcomings of the first plan, and the machinery for the planning was strengthened. The objective of the plan was to firmly establish Nigeria as a:

- united, strong, and self-reliant nation;
- great and dynamic economy;
- just and egalitarian society;
- land of bright and full opportunities; and
- free and democratic society.

These objectives were so fundamental to Nigeria's development that they were included in the 1979 constitution nine years later (Abasili, 2014).

The plan envisaged a rapid economic growth rate of 6.6 percent per annum, such that the national product can be doubled in fourteen years. It was emphatic on the need for rapid growth and progressive elimination of foreign dominance of the economy. According to Tekena et al. (1989), the planners, presumably the military rulers, were satisfied with the state taking command of the economy to achieve economic growth and self-reliance.

Fiscal policies were to be directed towards maximizing the flow of economic resources for economic development, while monetary policies were to be directed at maintaining confidence in the Nigerian currency through domestic wage and price stabilisation measures.

The plan did not achieve its objective of directing the programmes and budgets of the administration. Its main problems were poor implementation, insufficient funds, corruption, and the mono-cultural economy.

Despite these setbacks, the plan delivered on key projects and programmes like the National Youth Service Corps (NYSC), the introduction of the federal scholarship and loan scheme, and the construction of several roads.

Third National Development Plan (1975-1980)

This was the second development plan launched by the Yakubu Gowon-led military government. It came into being in April 1975 and was to run till March 1980. It anticipated an initial investment fund of N30 billion. Ayinla (1998) saw it as a watershed in the evolution of economic planning in Nigeria as, for the first time, extensive consultations were carried out with the private sector in the course of its preparation.

In July 1975, a new government took over the administration of the country. With the change came a reappraisal of the nation's priorities to better reflect the philosophy of the new administration. The new administration decided to emphasize projects in the areas of water supply, housing, agriculture and co-operatives, and health, which, by their very nature, have a direct bearing on the welfare of citizens as against prestigious projects of doubtful social relevance.

The government decided to increase the target number of hospital beds from the 87,000 originally approved in the plan document to 120,000 by 1980. Similarly, the projected units in the housing programme was increased to 200.000 housing units from 60,000.

This new scope for the housing sector entailed the construction of 30,000 housing units in Lagos and a maximum of 10,000 units at or near every state capital. With regards to water supply, the original target of 25 gallons per day per head of population set for the urban area was retained, while the scope of rural water supply schemes throughout the federation was to be doubled such that twice as many people and communities would have pipe-borne water by 1980. See appendix 3.

Administration

The cardinal principles of the plan included an increase in per capita income during the plan's period, more even distribution of income, reduction in the unemployment level, diversification of the economy, balanced development, and indigenisation of economic activities.

The plan was formulated and written by Nigerians, and it carried over the objectives of the second national development plan. By this time, the number of professional planners in the economic planning department had risen to one hundred and forty. In addition, the plan brought the indigenization of some categories of economic activities to the fore with the promulgation of the Nigeria Enterprises Promotion Decree of 1972.

Certain events of considerable national importance made the plan's review inevitable within a few months of its launch. First, the Yakubu Gowon administration was toppled in July 1975. Second, there was a sharp decline in the price of crude oil, Nigeria's major foreign exchange earner, between 1976 and 1976.

The crude oil output that reached a peak of 2.3 million barrels per day in October 1974 plummeted to 1.5 million barrels per day in May 1975, just two months after the launch of the third national development plan. Therefore, expected funding for the plan was greatly eroded.

The new government reappraised the nation's priorities to reflect its philosophy. It identified its new priorities as water supply, housing, agriculture, and health. In February 1976, the new government created seven new states and moved the federal capital from Lagos to Abuja. This reinforced the need to review the plan to accommodate the new realities as the new states needed new infrastructural facilities for their effective take-off. With the revision, the projected expenditure rose to N43 billion.

Another issue to consider was the level of oil output achieved in 1974. When the original plan was being prepared, it was based on the belief that there would be no financial constraints. However, no sooner had the plan been launched than the oil industry suffered a substantial decline in production and price. The crude oil output fell from a peak of 2.3 million barrels per day in October 1974 to 1.5 million barrels per day in May 1975, two months after launching the plan. Because of these reasons, the federal military government I October 1975 issued a directive that a review of the plan be effected.

Fourth National Development Plan (1981-1985)

The military administration of Murtala Muhammed and Olusegun Obasanjo issued guidelines for the fourth national development plan when it was about to leave office in 1979. The premise was that since Nigeria's primary objective was to achieve a rapid increase in the standard of living of the average Nigerian, every administration, whether military or civilian, should be pre-occupied with the realization of the objective. Therefore, the outgoing military regime felt it was its duty to prepare the ground adequately for the formulation of a new development plan.

The Shagari civilian administration was sworn in on October 1, 1979, with only six months left of the third development plan and the fourth's commencement. In October 1980, the government issued the outlines of the fourth national development plan (1981-1985). The plan is considerably bigger than all its predecessors with a projected capital expenditure of N82 billion. The public sector was to contribute N70.5 billion, while the private sector was to contribute N11.7 billion. It was the first time local governments participated as a distinct level of government with specific responsibilities and programmes.

Like its predecessors, the plan's preparation was centred in the national planning office of the federal ministry of national planning. Widespread consultations between the federal, states and local governments and the private sector were held in the preparation of the plan. For the first time, the private sector made inputs into Nigeria's national development plan.

Extensive consultations also took place between the officials of the National Planning Office and officials of other federal ministries and agencies and state ministries of economic planning during the plan's formulation. In addition, there were several meetings between officials and policy makers under the aegis of the Joint Planning Board, a conference of the minister and commissioners responsible for economic planning, and consultations between the National Planning Office and representatives of private-sector bodies such as the National Association of Chambers of Commerce, Industry, Mines and Agriculture and Manufacturing Association of Nigeria.

The plan was intended to further establish a solid base for the long-run economic and social development of Nigeria. It emphasized key sectors like agriculture, particularly food production, manufacturing, education, manpower development, and infrastructural facilities. Social services, especially housing and health, were also emphasized. A gross domestic growth rate of 7.2 percent was envisaged. It marked the beginning of the third decade of Nigeria's existence as an independent country.

The specific objectives of the fourth national development plan were:

- Increase in the real income of the average citizen.
- More even distribution of income among individuals and socio-economic groups.
- Reduction in the level of employment and under-employment.
- Increase in supply of skilled manpower.
- Reduction of the dependence of the economy on a narrow range of activities.
- Balanced development. That is, the achievement of a balance in the development of the different sectors of the economy and various geographical areas of the country.

- Increased participation by citizens in the ownership and management of productive enterprises.
- Greater self-reliance. That is, increased dependence on Nigerian resources in seeking to achieve the various objectives of the society. This also implies increased efforts to achieve the optimum utilization of our human and materials resources.
- Technological development.
- Increased productivity.
- Promoting a new national orientation is conducive to greater discipline, better attitude to work, and a cleaner environment.

In the context of the plan, agricultural production and processing enjoyed priority. A rapid growth in agricultural production was an essential component of the strategy of self-reliance, which was a major objective of the plan. Another priority area for the plan is education and manpower development. It was meant to tackle the shortage of skilled manpower in the country.

Housing, manufacturing and health constituted the next priority areas for the plan. Next in order of priorities was strengthening economic infrastructures, particularly power, water supply, and telecommunications. It was envisaged that the expansion of these facilities would be accompanied by increased emphasis on maintenance to ensure the effective realization of new and existing investments. With respect to land transportation, attention was to shift to the improvement of the railways. The planners envisaged that the construction of new standard gauge railway lines would commence alongside major improvements to existing lines to improve operational efficiency. The development of water transportation was also envisaged to receive increased attention, while the road sub-sector will see proper maintenance of the existing network.

The implementation of the fourth development plan, like its predecessor, was interrupted by a military change of governments, leading to poor performance of the economy (Salawu et al., 2012). The 1983 and 1985 coups saw different regimes at the helm of affairs of government. Coupled with this was the fluctuating price of crude oil, the mainstay of the economy. As a result, by the end of 1985, the actual revenues of the federal government were only 58.5 percent of the projected total for the period of the fourth national development plan.

It appears Nigerian national development plans have been hampered by future and external events, especially fluctuating oil prices (Ikeanyibe,

2009). The obvious explanation was that accurate and reliable forecasts were was not made by the planners. Fixed-term planning, as Okojie (2002) postulates, is inadequate for unstable economic and political societies.

At the end of the fourth plan's period, the foundation for sustainable growth and development was yet to be laid. The productive base of the economy and sources of Government revenue was yet to be diversified. The economy did not have its own driving force and was therefore highly susceptible to external shocks.

Odunlami (1999) posits that the fourth national development plan failed because the international market collapsed. It was built on a projection of 2.2 million barrels of crude oil per day and a projected price of $40 per barrel. Instead, the production level dropped sharply to an all-time low of 1.4 million barrels per day.

The situation was worsened by the rapid slide of the agricultural sector. Savings declined, unemployment rate rose, and the production capacity was grossly underutilized, leading to serious fiscal deficits. External debts shot up in the process with a severe shortage of foreign exchange.

The National Rolling Plans (1990-1998)

The Ibrahim Babangida administration (1985-1993) suspended long-term development plans, replacing them short-term ones referred to as rolling plans. This was done to hasten and facilitate economic growth.

Nnoli (1981) avers that the military ruler had argued that the new direction was informed by the need for Nigeria to exigently readjust its economic policies if it ever hopes to cope with the dynamic economic environment of the 1990s.

At the end of the fourth national development plan, Babangida instituted a one-year economic emergency programme to solve some of the obvious problems left behind by the Shagari administration. This programme was later absorbed by an economic policy called the Structural Adjustment Programme (SAP).

The administration believed that because the economy was highly indebted and in a parlous state, the basis for planning was eroded. Therefore, it chose SAP, a reform therapy of the World Bank and International Monetary Fund (IMF), intended to last for two years. The programme was, however, not realized within the time frame.

SAP underscored a shift from a project-based to a policy-based planning system. It emphasized a private sector-led economy, instead of the public sector-dominated economy of previous development plans.

SAP aimed to redress the basic structural imbalances in the economy, check its downward slide, establish a base for non-inflationary growth, and pursue policies that will encourage the emergence of a dynamic market-oriented economy.

The crisis that engulfed the Nigerian economy in the early 1980s required urgent institution of reforms. Bangura (1982) sees it as the most severe economic crisis experienced by the Nigerian state since its creation.

The Babangida administration preferred SAP to a loan from the IMF intended to lift the economy. It also ignored and jettisoned the short-term economic management programmes instituted by the Shagari and Buhari administrations, and the Economic Stabilisation (Temporary Provisions) Act.

According to Onoh (1983), the act prescribed reducing government expenditure and restricting imports. The administration consulted Nigerians on taking a loan from the IMF to bail the country out of its economic crisis. It was rejected by various interest groups. The government then opted for SAP on the understanding that it was the only alternative to the IMF loan.

At SAP's centre was the devaluation of the naira, subsidy removal, privatisation and commercialisation of public enterprises, trade liberalisation, the deregulation of prices and interest rates, removal of administrative controls, especially in foreign exchange transactions, reduction of public expenditure, and imposition of credit and economic squeeze (Olukoshi, 1993).

The rolling plans were meant to consolidate SAP gains and aid the economy's sustainable growth in the 1990s. Therefore, it was subjected to constant reviews based on the emerging realities within the period of implementation. It introduced what it referred to as new objectives, some short/medium term and some medium/long term. Some of the objectives are:

- Further promotion of non-oil exports.
- Increased self-sufficiency in food production.
- Further improvement of labour productivity through incentives.

- Substantial enlargement of the role of the private sector, including privatisation of some public enterprises.

The Babangida administration decided on a 20-year perspective plan for the period 1989-2008. According to the rolling plan's philosophy, the first phase of the perspective plan would constitute the fifth national development plan and be operated alongside the annual budget.

The first national rolling plan was adopted in 1990 and was meant to cover the period 1990-1992. According to the architects of this rolling plan programme, it was more suitable for an economy facing uncertainty and rapid change. The rolling plan was meant to be revised at the end of each year, at which point estimates, targets, and projects were added for an additional year. This means the planner revised the 1990-1992 three-year rolling plan at the end of 1990, issuing a new plan for 1991-93, and so on. In effect, as Ihonvbere (1991) observed, a plan is renewed at the end of each year, but the number of years remains the same as the plan rolls forward. In plainer language, as Okogie (2002) espoused, a three-tier planning system was to succeed SAP. The new proposal consisted of:

- a 15-20-year perspective or long-term plan;
- a three-year rolling plan; and
- an annual budget that will draw from the rolling plan.

Part of the progress said to have been made in the first year of the rolling plan's implementation was launching grassroots development programmes such as the Directorate of Foods, Roads and Rural Infrastructure (DFRRI), National Economic Reconstruction Fund, NERFUND, and rural electrification.

The second rolling plan (1991-1993), a roll-over from the first rolling plan, was also to help consolidate the gains of SAP with a target growth rate of 4.85 percent and 7.68 percent for the GDP on agriculture and manufacturing sectors, respectively. N161.1 billion was budgeted for the plan, with the federal government investing N83 billion.

The 1994-1996 plan was conceived to assuage Nigeria's boisterous macro-economic climate occasioned by the tense and uncertain political atmosphere that characterized the plan's period. The thrust was to facilitate the completion of unfinished projects through available resources. However, despite being reviewed annually since adoption, the rolling plans failed to meet the expectations of the government, its planners, and the larger society, partly, according to Odunlami (1999), due to its non-originality.

Aluko (1997) also asserts that the rolling plans were based on vulgar monetarism and crude medium-term financial strategies largely formulated and imposed from abroad. Okoji (2002) saw the rolling plans as no less than annual budgets since their preparation and revision was done on an almost yearly basis.

The same way the Babangida administration shelved the five-year development plan was the same way the Abacha administration jettisoned the rolling plan in 1996.

Before Abacha was the Ernest Shonekan transitory administration that came into office after Ibrahim Babangida was forced out.

Shonekan, a renowned technocrat, went about setting an agenda to find a lasting solution to Nigeria's economic problems. It took the form of an economic summit designed to provide a forum for both the public and private sectors to brainstorm on improving the Nigerian economy.

The first national economic summit, NES 1, took place in Abuja. According to Aluko-Olokun (1997), the summit achieved two key results: it provided a strong link between the public and private sector, and it brought articulated economic priorities.

It was the ideas from the next three economic summits that led to Vision 2010. Abacha started with some attempts at a populist regulation of the economy, after rejecting the SAP. As West (1997) observed, this did not fetch the expected dividends as shown by the 1.0 percent GDP growth rate in 1994, the worst in the history of Nigeria.

It did not take time for the government to begin to retrace its steps. A new economic initiative, "guided deregulation," was introduced. It consisted of a free market enterprise system with the private sector as its engine room. Its major principles were outlined in the 1995 budget with several efforts to improve the macro-economic environment. These efforts included the introduction of the foreign exchange monitoring decree, promulgation of the Nigerian Investment Promotion decree, sanitisation of the financial and banking system, and reduction of deficit financing.

Vision 2010

By early 1996, a basis of consistency in policy measures had been established with attendant stability in the macro-economy. The Third

Nigeria Economic Summit held in Abuja in September 1996. Its aim was to harness Nigeria's immense potentials for greater development. The summit shed more light on the visioning idea given by the second summit.

Abacha quickly bought into this vision. He accepted that Nigeria was ready to adopt a more systematic and carefully phased approach to its development. His predilection for 2010 as the target date for the proposed vision was due to its coincidence with Nigeria's fiftieth independence anniversary.

Vision 2010, deemed a collective vision for all Nigerians, was to promote a culture of long-term thinking and planning in Nigeria. On September 27, 1996, Abacha inaugurated the vision 2010 committee, which was given a 14-item term of reference. The terms can be grouped into three folds:

i. To constructively analyse why after more than 36 years of political independence, our development as a nation in many spheres has been relatively unimpressive, especially in relation to our potential.
ii. To envision or visualize where we would like to be at the time the nation will be a fifty-year-old country in 2010.
iii. To develop the blueprint and action plans for translating this shared vision into reality.

A 250-member committee of private sector representatives, government ministries, academics, journalists, traditional and trade union leaders, and foreign businessmen were given the mandate to draw up the vision document.

The composition of the committee was deliberate to represent the widest spectrum of stakeholder groups. It was headed by the former leader of the interim national government, Ernest Shonekan.

The committee set out to work after it was divided into various sub-groups. It operated from two coordinating secretariats, one in Lagos and the other in Abuja. The kernel of its debates was predicated on thirteen identified topics known as the critical success factors. They were grouped under the broad headings of human capital, value system, governing system, and global competitiveness.

The questions they set out to answer are:

- Where is Nigeria now?
- Where does she want to be?
- How will she get there?

The committee sought for and received inputs from all stakeholders, both at home and abroad. Opinion leaders and the grassroots, in particular, were not left out. Apart from soliciting for public memoranda and submissions on all aspects of the committee's terms of reference, a broad range of speakers from within and outside country, including virtually all the ministers and heads of key public agencies, were invited to address the committee. A wide array of workshops were also held to afford the generality of Nigerians the opportunity to make inputs into the report.

Using the concept of visioning, which has been successfully used for nation-building in other developing countries across the world, we have crafted a Vision for Nigeria based on the input received from broad segment of our people. We started out by thoroughly analysing the factors identified as being essential to a nation's success in today's world. We next defined the objectives together with the strategies to be used in achieving our shared aspirations. We also focused particular attention on implantation through the establishment of realistic blueprints, targets and action plans for realising our desires future. Our approach is detailed in part one of this final report. The above is as captured in the vision document.

Vision statement for Nigeria by year 2010 is:

> To be united, industrious, caring and god fearing democratic society committed to making the basic needs of life affordable for everyone and creating Africa's leading economy

From this vision statement, it can be seen that shared values centre on unity, industry, care for neighbours, religious and moral principles as well as a governing system rooted in the democratic process. These shared values provide the foundation upon which national success can be built.

Consequently, the twin challenges confronting Nigeria as a nation are to build on the foundation of our shared values in such a way that, by the year 2010, we will have, firstly, provided the minimum basic needs of life for all Nigerians and, secondly, become Africa's leading economy in all ramifications.

In order to realise vision 2010, ambitious, but nevertheless achievable targets for Nigeria in all areas including political, socio-cultural, and economic were set. It also set interim milestones for the years 2000 and 2005. This is to enable Nigeria focus on shorter term goals and thus, monitor progress towards achieving targets, and if necessary, make any mid-course corrections.

The vision as crafted by the committee is intended to serve as a compass to guide collective actions to reach targets by the year 2010. It envisages Nigeria can then plan for the period, 2020-2050, during which we should aim at joining the developed nations and in particular, the major powers which are responsible for shaping the future of the entire world. The vision 2010 targets may be said to be ambitious, but they are practical and achievable; they constitute a platform on which further sustainable development can be built throughout the entire 21st century.

The vision statement states that Nigeria shall be:

To be united, industrious, caring and god fearing democratic society committed to making the basic needs of life affordable for everyone and creating africa's leading economy

The vision challenges are:

To make the basic needs of life (water, food, health, housing and education) readily available and affordable for everyone;

To build and sustain a democratic society; and
To become Africa's leading economy.
The vision 2010 slogan is:
'A great Nigeria….is ours to build'.

The slogan presents both the promise of a Nigeria that is great and a call to duty for all Nigerians to join hands in building this great country. It asks Nigerians to take their destiny in their own hands and to rely more on themselves.

The elements of the vision statement give a vivid picture of Nigeria by the year 2010.

Nigeria is a nation of diverse cultures and languages, but united in the pursuit of one purpose- building of a stable, democratic, prosperous and great nation. Everyone, regardless of language, culture, ethnicity, religion, gender or status, sall be given equal opportunity and treated with fairness

The fundamental human rights of every Nigerians shall be acknowledged and respected. There shall be free movement of labour, goods and services. Excellence shall be encouraged and adequately rewarded.

A great Nigeria… is ours to build through unity

Nigeria is abundantly blessed with human and material resources. Nigerians belive in the dignity of labour and by their intellectual ability and hard work they will build a prosperous and great nation.

The government shall provide an enabling an environment for both indigenous and foreign entrepreneurs to exploit Nigeria's resources to the optimal advantage of all Nigerians.

Traditionally, the Nigerian society is a caring one, as exemplified by the extended family system in which every Nigerian is his brother's keeper. In the envisioned Nigeria this culture shall be sustained and good neighbourliness shall continue to prevail.

Nigeria freely elected leaders and the entire citizenry shall fear god and be overwhelmed by his awesomeness. They shall love him and obey his commandments. Nigerians shall be morally upright and willingly perform their civic duties

Nigeria shall be governed by leaders who are elected through a free and fair electoral process. These leaders shall be selfless and committed to the service of the people and shall be willing to sacrifice self-interest for the common good. All the three arms of government, the executive, legislature and judiciary, shall be independent and strong in the execution of their duties. They shall be supported by a free and responsible press and an enlightened citizenry.

The aspiration of every Nigerians is to afford the basic need of life. A united, industrious and caring Nigeria shall ensure that food, housing, water, primary health care service and quality education are available at affordable prices.

Nigeria is well endowed with natural and human resources. The enabling environment shall be improved to enhance the exploitation of these resources. Nigeria shall become Africa's leading economy.

The envisioned Nigeria shall be an industrial nation with the fastest economic growth rate in Africa over a sustained period, the highest ratio of manufacturing to GDP, the highest level of foreign reserves, the strongest currency and the highest quality of life on the continent.

For proper implementation of the Vision project, the report recommended that the following institutions be established:

I, The National Council on Nigerian Vision (NYNV) chaired by the Head of State. It should among other things carry out the following task:

- Supervise the implementation of the vision
- Ensure the harmonization of existing policy measures with the vision objectives and strategies
- Ensure effective and consistent dissemination of the vision to institutions and the wider public
- Establish strategic alliances and continue the process of continuous dialogue and consensus building with specialized constituencies such as traditional rulers, religious organizations, the civil service, private sector operatives and non-governmental organizations
- Co-ordinate and monitor all inter-sectoral related activities spanning rural development, poverty alleviation, water supply, urban and rural environmental sanitation, health, education, agriculture, control of population growth, electricity supply, communications, transportation, etc

Ii, The Nigerian Vision Foundation: government should promulgate legislation to create The Nigeria Vision Foundation, (NVF) to be run as a private institution.

Iii, The NCNV should be put in the schedule in the constitution of the Federal Republic of Nigeria.

The committee considered a similar vision in operation in Malaysia and used it as a case study. Experts from that country presented papers to the committee.

On September 30, 1997, the committee submitted its report. It proposed immediate, short-, medium-, and long-term measures to stimulate economic growth and transform Nigerians into patriotic citizens.

Its key recommendations are:

1. That government should focus on creating enabling environment that stimulates private sector savings and investments, provide conducive infrastructure, and govern effectively in public interests.
2. The private sector should support the government in a truly progressive partnership. It should also be the engine of growth of the economy.
3, Stable and consistent economic policies with emphasis on achieving low inflation rates and strong fiscal/monetary discipline.

The vision hopes Nigeria will, within the period it covers, achieve an annual GDP growth rate of 6-10 percent, inflation rate of not more than 3-5 percent by 2010, and a high level of employment.

The committee also recommended that another vision to plan for 2020-2050 to launch Nigeria into the league of developed countries be generated.

The following are the targets the vision set for itself:

- GDP growth rate of not less than 10 percent over the period till 2010.
- Inflation rate of less than 5 percent by 2010.
- Population growth rate of less than 2.0 percent per annum by 2010.
- Attain a ratio by Gross Domestic Savings to Gross Domestic Product of less than 30 percent (currently 9.5 percent).
- Share of education should not be less than 26 percent of the national budget, and not more than 20 percent of the education budget should be deployed for administrative expenses and overhead.
- Attract at least 10 percent of Direct Foreign Investment (DFI) to developing countries.
- Share of health in the federal budget should not be less than 10 percent and not more than 15 percent of this deployed as administration expenses and overhead.
- Balanced budget; Deficit (if at all) not to exceed 3 percent of the GDP.
- At least 50 percent local content of factor input in oil and gas activities by 2010.
- Fifty percent of aggregate downstream capital requirement to be locally sourced by year 2010.
- There should be 100 industrial clusters, each located near the primary raw material all over the country by year 2010.
- All gas flaring to stop by year 2010.
- Gas to be fuel of first choice for industry and household by 2010.
- Complete self-sufficiency in primary petro-chemicals production and substantial self-sufficiency in secondary petro-chemicals production.
- Agriculture and tourism as a major foreign exchange earners and large employers of labour.

- Self-sufficiency in the production of food, drugs, manufacture of beverages, textiles and building materials.
- Domestic self-sufficiency in the production and use of non-metal goods, basic chemicals, metal manufacturing and transport equipment by the year 2010.
- Acquisition, adaptation and mastery of technologies related to oil and gas, petro-chemicals and domestic manufacture and assembly of information technology, hardware/software by the year 2010.
- Acquisition, adaptation and mastery of high technology related to biotechnology, electronics and other electrical goods and solar energy by the year 2010.
- Human Development Index (HDI) to rise to 0.8 by the year 2010.
- Proven oil reserve to reach 40 billion barrels and production to reach 4 million barrels per day by the year 2010. The above is as captured in the vision document.

General Abacha did not waste much time in taking steps towards the implementation of Vision 2010. In November 1997, he established the National Council of Nigeria Vision (NCNV) to coordinate its implementation in line with its recommendations. It was to be carried out in three phases: short, medium, and long term. Practical implementation of the vision commenced with the 1998 and 1999 budgets. The sudden death of General Abacha, however, halted it.

The National Economic Empowerment and Development Strategy (NEEDS)

General Abdusalami Abubakar succeeded Abacha as Nigeria's head of state. His brief administration did not make any direct attempt to implement Vision 2010. Rather, Abubakar drew up a short-term rolling plan (1999-2001).

Democratic governance was restored in Nigeria on May 29, 1999, and in came the Olusegun Obasanjo administration. The new administration started with a four-year medium-term document known as the National Economic Direction (1999-2003). According to Donli (2008), its primary objectives included pursuing a strong, virile, and broad-based economy with adequate capacity to absorb externally generated shocks. These objectives were not much different from those of the Structural Adjustment Programme, but were entirely different from those of Vision 2010.

NEEDS is Nigeria homegrown poverty reduction strategy (PRSP). NEEDS was built on earlier efforts to produce an interim PRSP (I-PRSP) and the wide consultative and participatory process associated with it. NEEDS is not just a planner or paper founded on a clear vision, sound values, and enduring principles. It is a medium-term strategy (2003-2007) that derives from the country's long-term goals of poverty reduction, wealth creation, employment generation, and value re-orientation. NEEDS was a nationally coordinated framework of action in close collaboration with the state and local governments (with their state economic empowerment and development strategy, SEEDS) and other stakeholders to consolidate the achievements of the last four years (1999-2003) and build a solid foundation for the attainment of Nigerian's long-term vision of becoming the largest and strongest African economy and a key player in the global economy.

NEEDS rests on four key strategies: reforming the way the government and its institutions work; growing the private sector; implementing a social charter for the people; and re-orientation of the people with an enduring African value system.

Reforming the Government and its Institutions

The goal is to restructure, right-size, re-professionalise, and strengthen the government and public institutions to deliver and effective services to the people. It also aims to eliminate waste and inefficiency, and free up government resources for investment in infrastructure and social services. Key aspects of the institutional reforms include eradicating corruption, ensuring great transparency, promoting the rule of law, and stricter enforcement of contracts. In addition, an explicit service delivery program to re-orient government agencies toward effective delivery of services to the people was introduced.

In summary, the goal was to make government and public institutions serve the people; to make government play a developmental role rather than a haven for corruption and rent-seeking. The reforms at this level sought to ensure a predictable and sustainable macroeconomic framework, especially through a sustainable fiscal policy framework.

Growing the Private Sector

NEEDS was a development strategy anchored on the private sector as the engine of growth for wealth creation, employment generation, and poverty reduction. The government is the enabler, the facilitator, and the regulator, while the private sector is the executor, the direct investor, and manager of businesses. The key elements of this strategy were renewed privatisation, deregulation and liberalisation programmes (to shrink the domain of public sector and buoy up the private sector); infrastructure development, especially electricity and transport; explicit sectorial strategies for agriculture, industry/SMEs; services (especially tourism, art and culture, and information/communication technology), oil and gas, and solid minerals. Other agenda elements include the mobilisation of long-term capital for investment, appropriate regulatory frameworks, a coherent and consistent trade policy and regional/global integration regime, and specific interventions to encourage the development of some sectors. For instance, to enhance rapid industrial growth and efficient exploitation of resources, the government would encourage strong linkages between science and technology parks (STPs), industry, and R&D institutions. In addition, there shall be deliberate efforts to promote technology acquisition from within and across national boundaries.

In collaboration with the states, a key strategy was to promote the emergence and flourishing of industrial clusters. In a global economy characterized by increasing agglomeration of industries, promoting clusters to ensure economies of scale is an important strategy. The small and medium enterprises (SMEs) are critical for employment generation, and therefore received special attention under NEEDS. In addition, NEEDS sought to promote the emergence of medium and large commercial farms, plantations, and industrial conglomerates that would harness the economies of scale and effectively compete in today's global market.

Implementing a Social Charter

NEEDS claimed to be about people, their welfare, health, education, employment, poverty-reduction, empowerment, security, and participation. This is the overarching goal of NEEDS. With 50 percent of the population school-age children, NEEDS viewed education as the most important bridge to the future and a powerful instrument of empowerment.

The HIV/AIDS epidemic is not just a social problem, it is a major threat to productivity and the economy. Effective healthcare delivery systems, especially those directed at combating the scourge of HIV/AIDS and other preventable diseases (malaria and tuberculosis), are key strategies for preserving a healthy workforce. Explicit programmes were directed at youth re-orientation and employment. The existing pension scheme was to be replaced by a contributory pension scheme to give senior citizens a better life after retirement. Under NEEDS, reforms were proposed to promote the emergence of a vibrant mortgage and housing development system led by private farmers. This is a key element of the poverty reduction strategy since over 50 percent of the poor are in agriculture. The continuing investment in water resources not only provides a key social service—water to the people—it also provides irrigation for increased agricultural productivity. The industry, especially the SMEs, is expected to boost employment, particularly the urban labour force. In collaboration with the states (under SEEDS) and local governments, an integrated rural development programme was a major strategy to stem the rural-urban migration. Another key strategy of the social charter was inclusiveness and empowerment. This was not just on the economic front, but deliberate programmes to give voice to the weak and the vulnerable groups through increased participation in decision-making and implementation, and laws and programmes to empower women, children, the handicapped, and the elderly. For example, NEEDS aimed for a minimum of 30 percent representation for women in all aspects of national life wherever feasible.

Value Re-orientation

The key message of those that put the NEEDS document together was 'it is not business as usual.' The privatisation programme was designed to shrink the domain of the state and hence the pie of distributable rents that have been the haven of public sector corruption and inefficiency. It was geared to push thousands of appointed board members of parastatals into productive engagements. The public sector reforms aimed to emphasise professionalism, selfless service, and efficiency (value-for-money), anti-corruption measures, fight against advance fee fraudsters, and strive towards greater transparency in public and private sector financial transactions to ensure accountability, and send the message that those who make money through illegal and illegitimate means have no hiding place. A further part of the reform agenda was ensuring hard work was rewarded and corruption and rent-seeking were punished. The people wlere to be empowered to hold public officials accountable through some bill of rights (especially the right to information act), and mobilized to re-emphasize the virtues of honesty, hard work, selfless service, moral rectitude, and patriotism. The national orientation agency (NOA) and its state counterparts were to be strengthened to actively lead the campaign. The government would also encourage civil society, community-based, non-governmental, private sector, and religious and socio-cultural-traditional organisations to provide leadership in the campaign for a new value system. Agencies and organisations would be encouraged to take specific steps to reward excellence as the demonstration effect could help to motivate the imitation of exemplary behaviour by others.

Implementation of NEEDS

Over the years, ineffective implementation of economic development plans have been a major issue. NEEDS was envisaged to be different: it was a plan on the ground. There were a number of government programmes with policy thrusts consistent with those of NEEDS. The president headed the coordination of the implementation and there is a systematic process of monitoring and evaluation. At the federal level, commitment to the implementation of NEEDS is total. There was to be periodic (quarterly) review of performance-----assessment of achievements, constraints and prospects. In addition, there was an independent monitoring committee made up of men and women of sterling qualities most of whom were directly involved in the reform process and reported directly to the president based on targets and objectives set for the various reforms. The National Assembly also played constructive and complementary oversight roles.

A key element of the implementation is a system of collaboration and coordination between the federal and state governments, donor agencies (through effective donor coordination), the private sector, civil society, NGOs, and other stakeholders. Given Nigeria's federal structure and the fact state and local governments will increasingly control more resources than the federal government, only a coordinated approach can produce the intended results. All the statutory institutions for inter-government coordination of development programmes, such as the national council on education, health, and agriculture were to be more proactive in coordinating sectoral strategies.

Furthermore, NEEDS required a heavy investment programme to jumpstart the economy in a pro-poor and poverty-reducing manner. Aside from the projected investment by the federal and state governments and the private sector, there was still a financial gap that required special efforts to mobilize the required finance. Therefore, the president set up a standing committee on funds mobilization to assist in mobilizing the required funds.

The discarding of the vision came to some observers as a big shock. Uzor (2012) asserts that the decision by the Obasanjo administration to discontinue the implementation of the vision cannot be rationalized as it remains one of the best economic development blueprints any government can produce anywhere in the developing world.

He argues that a collection of very credible experts took out quality and painstaking time to draw up the vision, and no wise and imaginative leader would throw such a blueprint away.

The new plan did not achieve its target of deregulating the economy, reducing bureaucratic red-tapes in governance, alleviating poverty, and providing infrastructural and welfare programmes.

When the government was re-elected in 2003, it came up with another approach to development planning. It thought of a comprehensive socio-political and economic reform that will come with radical changes in the conduct of the government's business. This thinking gave birth to the New Economic Empowerment and Development Strategy (NEEDS).

NEEDS was seen as Nigeria's plan for prosperity. It was a four-year medium-term plan for the period 2003-2007. The NEEDS document (2002) was based on the constitution, the Kuru declaration, previous initiatives such as the Vision 2010, and nationwide consultation.

The economic development strategy was to consolidate on the achievements of the Obasanjo administration between 1999 and 2003 and lay a solid foundation for sustainable poverty reduction, employment generation, wealth creation, and value re-orientation.

NEEDS was based on the notion that these goals can only be achieved by creating an environment in which businesses can thrive. It was intended to offer farmers better equipment, seedlings, and other forms of support to boost their productivity.

Improvement in education and health care delivery was also on the cards. The NEEDS programme also sought to replace the old pension scheme with a contributory one. It created room for synergy between the federal and state governments. The state and local governments were expected to institute a similar strategy—the States Economic Empowerment and Development Strategy (SEEDS) and the Local Economic Empowerment and Development Strategy (LEEDS)—with a minimum set of targets and priorities. NEEDS targeted a minimum GDP growth rate of 5 percent in 2005, 6 percent in 2005 and 2006, and 7 percent in 2007.

To finance the programme, the Obasanjo administration hoped to free up funds by curbing wasteful ventures, selling assets, reforming the tax system, increasing resource use efficiency, mobilizing domestic savings, attracting foreign direct investments and overseas development assistance, and debt relief from creditors.

Under NEEDS, substantial progress was made in the introduction of structural reforms in the economy. They include a comprehensive reform of the banking sector and its consolidation, growth in the non-oil sector, fight against corruption, and the introduction of the Dutch auction system for foreign exchange trading.

International financial institutions like the World Bank commended the nigerian government for formulating and implementing a programme like NEEDS. The development of the strategy enjoyed strong ownership and underscored the commitment of the Nigerian government to an ambitious plan that aims to put it on the path to sustainable growth and poverty reduction (World Bank, 2005). The World Bank recognized that it was a significant shift from Nigeria's previous agenda.

However, the blueprint came under heavy criticism from scholars. Ikeanibe, (2009) argues that while Nigeria's economy grew within the period of its implementation, with the country's budget crossing the multibillion-naira threshold, poverty in the country was also on the rise. In the same period; approximately 70 percent of the population was living on less than $1 per day.

He argues further that since wealth and employment creation are key objectives of the plan, its inability to achieve both equals colossal failure.

NEEDS also failed to meet its infrastructural development objective. Inspite of the huge funds allocated to power generation and road construction, general decay rather than improvement was noticeable.

NEEDS emphasised a private sector-led economy, which violates the Nigerian Constitution that classifies the country as a mixed economy. In addition, market reforms were pursued without the safety nets contained in the document.

In the late days of the Obasanjo administration, efforts were made to draw the second leg of the NEEDS document, NEEDS II. A draft of the document was presented to stakeholders in Lagos on May 3, 2007, four weeks before the end of the administration's tenure. It identified Nigeria's developmental challenges as growth without employment, high poverty levels, poor infrastructure, and the poor energy situation.

Vision 20:2020

The idea for Vision 20:2020 can be traced to a 2005 report by Goldman Sachs, an international investment banking group. The report summarised the overall structural conditions and policy settings for countries globally. The report's analysis focused on the BRIC countries (Brazil, Russia, India, and China). The report stated that the prospects of a country's ability to meet its growth potentials depend on 13 sub-indices that can be grouped into five basic areas:

i.   Macro-economic stability: Inflation, government deficit, external debt.
ii.   Macro-economic conditions: Investment rate, openness of the economy.
iii. Technological capabilities: Penetration of PCs, phones, internet.
iv.   Human capital: Education, life expectancy.
v.   Political conditions: Political Stability, rule of law, corruption.

Considering the factors above, the group listed the possible 20 largest world economies by 2025 if the right policy measures are instituted and good mechanisms put in place. Nigeria was placed on this list.

According to the projection, Nigeria would overtake countries like Spain, Belgium, Poland, The Nordic Countries, Israel, Romania, South Africa, and Egypt by 2020. The Goldman Sachs report viewed the BRIC countries as the most likely to meet its predictions and believed only two African countries—Nigeria and Egypt—will have a GDP higher than Italy's by 2015.

The Obasanjo administration saw the report as an opportunity to launch a new economic development strategy for Nigeria with 2020 as its target date. According to Soludo (2007), the government built the new idea around a delivery vehicle specially designed by the top brass of the Central Bank of Nigeria (CBN) known as the Financial System Strategy 2020.

The strategy sought to create a robust and vibrant financial system that can power the economy to greater heights. It envisaged a vibrant economy that will propel those of other African countries. It came with extensive reforms of the banking sector. as mega banks were created and small banks encouraged to merge to achieve a capital base of $200 million and above.

The framework for the Vision 20:2020 strategy was still being worked out when the tenure of the Obasanjo-led administration ended. Then, the Umar Yar'Adua-led administration was sworn in, and the responsibilities for its development fell to it and the Goodluck Jonathan-led administration.

Again, the organized private sector, in the form of the Nigerian Economic Summit Group, was on hand to chart the course for the new strategy. At its 2007 summit, the strategy was its central theme, with presentations by officials of Goldman Sachs on its workability.

The Yar'Adua administration ensured that the vision encapsulated the key thrusts and principles of NEEDS and its own agenda as contained in the seven-point agenda. The development of the vision commenced with the approval of its framework by the Federal Executive Council in 2009. At its apex was the national council on Vision 20:2020, which was given the mandate to spearhead the development and implementation of the vision in collaboration with the National Planning Commission.

The visioning process drew some levels of participation from a broad spectrum of Nigerians, ranging from the private sector to top public servants, and from development partners to members of various non-governmental organisations.

It commenced with the development of comprehensive strategic development plans for each sector of the economy after detailed diagnostic assessment and visioning sessions. The country was analysed across 29 thematic areas for this purpose, and the efforts was delivered through 29 National Working Technical Groups (NTWGs), comprising leading experts on each thematic area.

The areas are agriculture, business environment and competitiveness, corporate governance, culture, tourism and national orientation, education, employment, energy, environment, financial sector, foreign policy, governance, health, housing and human development.

Others are ICT, manufacturing, media and communications, Niger delta and regional development, political system, security, SME's, sports development, trade and commerce, transport, urban and rural development, and water and sanitation.

Each group submitted strategic plans that included objectives, priorities, and sector-specific visions. This exercise was replicated at the state level and in different MDAs by stakeholder development committees (SDAs).

The NTWGs and SDCs were complemented by twelve special interest groups (SIGs) to ensure all perspectives were included in the visioning process. The SIGs included the legislature, judiciary, media, and other interest groups.

Two working groups were constituted to develop the final blueprint. The first working group was mandated to develop a consistent macro-economic framework to underpin the vision. The second, the central working group, was mandated to develop the first draft of the Vision 20:2020 economic transformation plan across the three broad themes defined as the central thrusts of the vision.

After nine months of intensive work by over 1,000 experts, the government, on September 24, 2009, unveiled the draft vision document for stakeholders to vet. The final document was approved for implementation by the Federal Executive Council on October 14, 2009.

The vision's main objective was to launch Nigeria into the top 20 largest world economies by 2020. It aimed to achieve this with a minimum GDP of $900 billion and a per capita income of $4,000 or more per annum. This implies that the country's economy must grow at an average of 13.8 percent over the course of the vision's implementation.

The vision had two broad objectives: optimizing human and natural resources to achieve rapid economic growth, and translating that growth into equitable social development for all citizens. These aspirations are defined across four dimensions: the social, economic, institutional, and environmental dimensions.

Social Dimension

A peaceful, equitable, harmonious, and just society, where every citizen has a strong sense of national identity, and are supported by an educational and healthcare system that caters for all and sustains a life expectancy of not less than 70 years.

Economic Dimension

A globally competitive economy that is resilient and diversified with a globally competitive manufacturing sector that is tightly integrated and contributes no less than 25 percent of the Gross Domestic Product.

Institutional Dimension

A stable and functional democracy where the rights of the citizens to determine their leaders are guaranteed, and adequate infrastructure is in place to support a market-friendly and globally competitive business environment.

Environmental Dimension

A level of environmental consciousness that enables and supports sustainable management of the nation's God-given natural endowments to ensure their preservation for the benefit of present and future generations.

Two planned departures from the past underpin the success of Vision 20:2020: integrating sectoral planning and adopting a cluster-based approach to industrialization.

The economic transformation strategy for Vision 20:2020 is anchored on three overarching thrusts:

1. Creating the platform for success by urgently and immediately addressing the most debilitating constraints to Nigeria's growth and competitiveness;
2. Forging ahead with diligence and focus in developing the fabric of the envisioned economy by:
   i. *Aggressively pursuing a structural transformation from a mono-product economy to a diversified, industrialized economy;*

ii.   *Investing to transform the Nigerian people into catalysts for national growth and renewal, and a lasting source of comparative advantage; and*

iii.   *Investing to create an environment that enables the co-existence of growth and development on an enduring and sustainable basis.*

3.   Developing and deepening government's capacity to consistently translate national strategic intent into action and results by instituting evidence-based decision-making in Nigeria's public policy space.

The identified policy measures that the vision focused on are a shift from the revenue allocation mechanism of sharing the cake to baking it, intensification of the war against corruption, private sector lead to increase non-oil sector growth, investments in human capital development, entrenching merit as a fundamental principle and core value, addressing threats to national security, and deepening reforms in the social sector, as well as extending reforms to sub-national levels.

The Vision 20:2020 document explains the basis for the economic indices target it set for itself for 2020. It was hinged on a dynamic comparative analysis of Nigeria's potential growth rate vis-à-vis those of other top 40 economies.

For the GDP for instance, the growth requirements were determined by ascertaining the current GDPs of the bottom five members of the current top 20 economies and using their average growth rates to project what their GDPs would be in 2020. The estimates show that by 2020, Poland and Indonesia will have GDP sizes close to Nigeria's aspiration of at least $900bn.

For Nigeria to achieve Poland's economic size (GDP of US$ 963 billion), it will have to grow at an annual average rate of 13.4 percent. To achieve Indonesia's GDP value ($1.05 trillion), the Nigerian economy must grow at an annual average rate of 13.7 percent till 2020. Given the similarities between the Nigerian and Indonesian economies at a time, Indonesia's projected economic size was used as a benchmark. Therefore, the targeted average annual growth rate was 13.8 percent. Realizing this quantum leap in Nigeria's economic growth would require a fundamental change in the economy's structure from primary production (agriculture and crude oil production) to industrial manufacturing and services.

Unsurprisingly, Nigeria exhibits the features of an underdeveloped country, while the top 20 countries by GDP exhibit the features of developing or developed economies. In three of the countries, agriculture contributes between 3 and 5 percent of GDP, compared to Nigeria's 42 percent. Worse still, Nigeria's agricultural sector has a much lower productivity rate.

Based on the features and development trajectories of the top 20 economies, Nigeria has to aspire to have a more realistic economic structure. This desired structure of the economy should see the relative contribution of agriculture decline to perhaps 15 percent over the long term, while the sector's productivity steadily increases. Simultaneously, the industrial sector must be propelled to drive the economy over the medium term till 2015, while a transition to a service-based economy is envisaged from 2018 to 2020.

However, for the required structural transformation to occur, the binding constraints on the agricultural and industrial sectors must be addressed, particularly the infrastructure bottleneck.

One of the critical policy frameworks that the vision identified is the expansion of investments in critical infrastructure. It highlighted encouraging private investments as a means of achieving this. Emphasis was on building on the framework for infrastructure concession where private sector organisations will be allowed to build, maintain, rehabilitate, operate, transfer or own public infrastructure.

Four clear imperatives were included to guarantee the realization and implementation of the vision. First, they are linked to existing mechanisms for execution (medium-term development plans and expenditure framework, medium-term sector strategies, and annual budgets). Second, institutionalising monitoring and evaluation across all levels of government to improve their capacity to translate all strategic plans and programmes into outcomes and impacts. The third is the deployment of legislations to ensure adherence to the plan and institutionalising specific reforms recommended in the plan, one of which is the Fiscal Responsibility Act. The last is defining a clear strategy for mobilising the citizenry towards greater demand for performance and accountability using the vision as a guiding light.

The implementation of the plan was anchored on three medium-term sub-plans. These plans highlighted the government's socio-economic and infrastructure development priorities.

The first plan covered 2010-2013, the second 2014-2017, and the third 2018-2020. The plans were designed as a policy and strategy-oriented blueprint to steer the implementation of development interventions in the years leading to 2020.

It articulates projects and programmes for the key sectors of the Nigerian economy, and critical policy priorities. It also has an in-built mechanism for monitoring and evaluating progress against set targets.

The first implementation plan put aggregate investment projections at N32 trillion: N10 trillion from the federal government, N9 trillion from the state governments, and N13 trillion from the private sector.

It also detailed specific goals, strategies, and performance targets for all sectors of the economy in line with the vision's strategy. The medium-term expenditure framework was used to link policy, planning, and budgeting across all government levels.

Actual implementation of the vision started with the 2010 budget. This was monitored and evaluated by the National Planning Commission (NPC), while a minister who doubled as the deputy chairman headed the team. A monitoring and evaluation office was created to anchor the overall coordination of the national monitoring and evaluation system. The team also had to prepare and submit annual national reports to the Office of the President and the National Assembly, alongside executive summaries.

Other institutions in the Vision document with monitoring and evaluation functions are the Budget Office, the Budget Monitoring And Price Intelligence Unit (now the Bureau of Public Procurement), the Office of the Secretary of the Government of the Federation, the National Poverty Eradication Programme, and the oversight committees of the National Assembly. The situation at the state level is similar to that of the federal level, although there are differences from state to state.

For legal frameworks that will ensure compliance with the implementation guidelines of the vision, a bill to enact the vision as a law was to be forwarded to the National Assembly. The bill, the Nigerian National Development Plan, was drafted by the Federal Law Reform Commission and it sought punitive consequences for non-compliance. The consequences included a prohibition from access to the federation account and other consolidated revenues.

Another law considered was one mandating the president to present the annual national performance report to a joint session of the National Assembly. Others are the Freedom of Information Act, the Development Planning Act, the Project Implementation Continuity Act, and the Arbitration and Conciliation Act and Rules.

Other legislative considerations and actions to support the implementation of the Vision 20:2020 were amendments to existing laws:

- The Fiscal Responsibility Act
- The Public Procurement Act
- Land Use Act
- Companies and Allied Matters Act
- Banking and Other Financial Matters Act (BOFIA)
- Evidence Act

Certain parts of the Nigerian Constitution were slated for amendments to guarantee the successful implementation of the vision. They are the portions that have a bearing on appropriation. The provisions include sections 80, 81, 82, and 83, which deal with finance and expenditure to achieve a more bottom-up approach to budgeting and greater involvement of communities and stakeholders in the budgeting process. Amendments were also made to the exclusive and concurrent lists (second schedule: legislative powers) to enable the implementation of proposed reforms in the police, prisons, railways, and revenue allocation.

The Seven-point Agenda

The seven-point agenda was the medium-term economic development blueprint of the Umar Musa Yar'Adua government. It was meant to be in place for four years and was hugely influenced by two distinct documents: The National Economic Empowerment and Development Strategy (NEEDS) and the 2007 manifesto (programme implementation) of the Peoples Democratic Party (PDP). It articulates policy priorities that will strengthen reforms and build the Nigerian economy to enable gains felt by the people.

It further provided an unambiguous answer to "how" the campaign promises predicated on the agenda can translate into widespread economic gains and democratic dividends for citizens.

The priority areas were:

- Sustainable growth in the real sector of the economy
- Physical infrastructure: (power, energy, and transportation)
- Agriculture
- Human capital development (education and health)
- Security, law, and order
- Combating corruption
- Niger-Delta development

The philosophy behind the agenda was for Nigeria to determine where it is, where it wants to be and where it should be. Therefore, the common man was placed at the centre of development efforts by the plan to make citizens beneficiaries of the country's resources.

The agenda set immediate policy directions for the Yar' Adua government to deepen reforms right from the outset. They included:

- Declaration of emergency in the power sector
- Constitute a credible economic team
- Present prioritised supplementary budget
- Commit to fiscal responsibility
- Commit to prudent borrowing policy
- Initiate a land reform process
- Review and adopt NEEDS II document
- Pursue the implementation of reviewed trade policy

The agenda also committed to what it referred to as a responsive social policy that included the following:

- Develop and launch marshal plan for Niger-Delta development.
- Enhance rate of investment in education, health, and infrastructure.
- Immediately resolve ASUU strike and other labour-related issues.

The agenda also made provisions for what it termed "A Clean Government."

- Commit to the rule of law.
- Constitute a qualitative cabinet guided by ethical codes.
- Asset declaration by the president and the entire cabinet members.
- Demonstrate commitment to transparency in areas such as:

1. Government finance
2. Oil bloc allocation
3. Fertilizer distribution
4. Sale of public enterprises.

- Initiate comprehensive electoral reforms.

- All major appointments, policies, contracts taken after the election to be reviewed.
- Increase women's representation in government.
- Grant presidential amnesty to Niger-Delta militants and other political detainees.

The seven-point agenda listed targets it intends to achieve in the first 100 days of the Yar'Adua administration. They came in sub-categories.

Job Creation

- Focus on private-public partnership (PPP) as a key tool for infrastructure development.
- Develop a comprehensive SME framework.

- Have a comprehensive back-to-farm programme and aggressive tree planting campaign.
- Effectively implement local content policy in the oil and gas industry.
- After investment guidelines for pension firms in favour of real sector and housing
- Commit to building gas infrastructure (pipelines) to increase gas utilisation in the country.
- Introduce manufacturing expansion grant.

Improving the Living Conditions of All Nigerians

- Support four-year mass housing schemes through aggressive mortgage finance.
- Enhance enrolment in primary and secondary schools.
- Increase resource allocation for universal access to cost-effective relevant health services.
- Design an institutional framework for evaluation of social and economic programmes which will report directly to the president
- Coordinate efforts to roll back poverty through fiscal and monetary policies that are self-reinforcing and with positive feedback on PPP.

Genuine National Reconciliation/Institutional Reforms

- Accelerate the ongoing reforms of the police, prisons, the judicial system, and all other government institutions.
- Strengthen the effectiveness of the Nigerian Police.

The agenda listed areas of focus after the first year. They are:

Sustainable Growth

- Promote sustainable large-scale commercial agriculture based on plantation economy, cash crops, orchards, irrigation, and proteins production.
- Increase public and private sector investment in agriculture R&D.
- Evolve ways of encouraging the flow of capital to the real sector of the economy.
- Boost power generation by building more hydro and coal power plants.
- Link the evolving housing market needs with capital market to raise homeownership rate.

Strengthening Human Development

- Embark on a comprehensive reform of tertiary institutions.
- Sustain increased funding of primary and secondary level of education.
- Sustain increased funding provision of basic health services.
- Resolve dysfunctional educational system.

A Functional Government

- Introduce nationwide community policing.
- A comprehensive review of bankruptcy and insolvency laws and strengthening of foreclosure procedure.
- Deepen expenditure management reform.

For the mid-term, the agenda outlined the following targets:

Long-term Development

- Emphasise biotechnology and genetically modified foods (GMF) to boost food supply.
- Launch new targeted investment drives in specific industries where competitive advantages exist.
- Establish and adopt a routine process to annually meet JV cash calls in the oil and gas industry.
- Expand rail and road network and maintain existing infrastructure.
- Strategic development of mineral resources.
- Establish a comprehensive set of fiscal incentives to encourage the development of high potential industries.
- Evolve ways to enhance all-season farming through irrigation.
- Encourage links between formal and informal sectors of the economy.
- Sustain the development of rural infrastructure.
- Tackle environmental degradation.

Sustainable Social Programmes

- Expand the coverage of health insurance and provision of basic health care for all.
- Create a youth development fund for capacity building.
- Help the poor to broaden their asset base and increase access to financial services.

Quality Service Delivery

Accelerate implementation of:

- E-government agenda
- Civil service reforms
- Reform and modernise the judiciary
- Property rights and land tenancy (legal and regulatory framework)
  The final targets set by the agenda are those that should count at the end of the administration's four-year tenure (2007-2011).

A More Prosperous Economy

- A country with a high credit rating.
- Functional and efficient infrastructure.
- Efficient and adequate power supply.
- Adequate supply of refined petroleum products (emphasis on local refineries) and doubling of local content in the oil and gas industry.
- Significantly reduced cost of doing business.

Substantial Progress towards Achieving the MDGs

- Substantial reduction in the number of people living below the poverty line and income inequality.
- Eradicate preventable diseases.
- Easier access to anti-retroviral drugs.
- Achieving environmental sustainability.
- Eliminating gender disparity in primary and secondary education.

A More Stable Polity

- A country based on law and order and a disciplined society.
- Lower corruption-transparency index.
- Responsive, ethical and efficient civil service.
- Corruption-free and efficient judicial system.
- Adoption of true fiscal federal structure; allocate revenue to different tiers of government commensurate with powers.

The Transformation Agenda

This was the economic development plan of the Goodluck Jonathan administration (2011-2015). It draws from and is based on the Vision 20:2020 economic development plan. The idea was to deepen the implementation of the Vision and provide a sense of direction for the Jonathan administration.

It is based on a set of priority policies and programmes that will transform the economy when implemented. A presidential committee was set up to scrutinise the document, after which it got a presidential endorsement.

The document identified key policies and programmes to be delivered during the administration's tenure, have them phased out, and propose a suitable monitoring mechanism.

The Transformation Agenda proposed a GDP growth rate of 11.7 percent for the period. The policymakers hoped that will translate to real and nominal GDP of N428.6 billion and N73.2 trillion for the period. It is worth stating that this is the same target set by the Vision 20:2020 economic development plan. So, one can argue that it is a derivative of the economic development blueprint.

A total investment size of N40.75 trillion in nominal terms was projected for the programme's period. While the public sector was expected to contribute N24.45 trillion or 60 percent, the private sector was expected to contribute N16.30 trillion or 40 percent.

The Agenda provided key policies to be pursued by the government. They are: ensuring greater harmony between fiscal and monetary policies, pursuit of sound macro-economic policies, including fiscal prudence supported by monetary policies to contain inflation, the budget process should be reviewed to provide greater clarity of the roles between the executive and legislature. The policy's direction drew inspiration from the US system and concentrates on setting allocation priorities rather than micro-budgeting or contesting figures with the executive.

On job creation, the Agenda identified some policy measures that will be pursued. They include:

- Implementing a youth employment safety support programme that includes conditional cash transfer and vocational training.
- Development of industrial clusters.
- Reviewing of university curricula to align with industry job requirements and promotion of apprentice/work experience programmes and joint ventures.
- Enforcement of mandatory sub-contracting and partnering with locals by foreign construction companies.
- Implementation of mandatory skills transfer to Nigerians by foreign construction companies.

The Agenda identified some other short-term policy measures. They are:

- Limiting total recurrent spending as a percentage of GDP to 6 percent from the current 8.5 percent, while increasing capital expenditure as a percentage of GDP from 4 to 6.5 percent in 2011 (and rising significantly thereafter).

- Aligning recurrent expenditure with non-oil revenue and devoting a substantial proportion of oil revenue to capital expenditure.

The Agenda, however, hopes to, in the long term, demonstrate adequate political will to deepen accountability and transparency in the oil industry and pursue reforms in the sector to reduce the cost of production. It also made provision for early engagement of interest groups in the budgeting process.

The agenda also targeted a governance process that will enthrone more effective and efficient use of public resources, proper financial management, and fiscal prudence.

The Transformation Agenda also contained policy thrusts for achieving greater efficiency and independence in the judiciary through funding, capacity building, elimination of corruption, and increased professionalism. On foreign policy, the Agenda sought greater funding and rationalisation of the number of missions. For the legislature, the Agenda had a policy thrust that would facilitate the creation of a dynamic, constitutionally effective, public and responsive legislature that is proactive in its legislative duties, independent and aware of its constitutionally prescribed roles and partnership with other arms of government.

The Transformation Agenda's policy thrust for human capital development was vast. For example, on education, it sought to promote primary enrolment of all children of school-going age, irrespective of the income profile of the parents, provision of infrastructure, and enhancement of efficiency, resourcefulness, and competence and capacity building of teachers.

On the health sector, the Transformation Agenda incorporated the policy thrust of the Vision 20:2020 economic development plan as it concerns the health sector and captured in the National Strategic Health Development Plan (NSHDP). The plan was a pact between Nigeria and its development partners on health care issues.

On Electricity infrastructure, the Transformation Agenda proposed a total investment outlay of 1.896 trillion Naira for the period, 2011-2015. This covers investments in four keys areas of power generation, transmission, distribution and alternative energy.

The strategies to be adopted in achieving the objective of increasing electricity supply are deregulation of the industry, enthroning a commercial tariff regime and a limited transmission loss within the sector.

On ICT, the agenda proposed an investment outlay of 22.2 billion Naira over the period 2011-2015 with a policy thrust of establishing a national knowledge based economy, a favorable investment climate driven by a PPP arrangement.

For transportation, the Transformation Agenda proposed a total investment of approximately 4.465 trillion Naira for the period between 2011 and 2015. It will cover roads, railways, inland waterways, ports and airport development.

The main policy thrust is to evolve a multimodal, integrated and sustainable transport system. Again, Public-Private Partnership is to push it through.

The Transformation Agenda listed key priority programmes and projects to be executed during its life span. 1613 of them were listed in 20 MDAs and sectors. 385 of them, constituting 22 percent of the total are new, while 1361, that's about 78 percent are on-going.

The Transformation Agenda has in built mechanism for implementation strategy, its funding, as well as monitoring and evaluation. Its financing was based on three broad categories. They are on-budget, off-budget and private sector resources.

The MDAs were responsible for executing policies and programmes, with ministers and CEOs taking the driver's seat. It also planned to adopt the cluster approach in order to promote regional economies and products in terms of comparative costs basis.

It also planned that economic coordination be undertaken at three levels: planning, policy and programmes at the institutional level, coordination at the level of MDAs and three tiers of government (NPC, NEC, FEC) and at the states and local governments and at the sector level (SPBs, SECs).

For monitoring and evaluation, the Agenda adopted the framework established by the Vision 20:2020 economic development plan and its first national implementation plan (2011-2013) in monitoring its implementation and performance.

It listed agencies and bodies that would undertake programme monitoring, including the National Assembly, the Ministry of Finance, the M and E office in the presidency (Economic Intelligence Office), and the National Planning Commission (NPC). The NPC was to oversee and coordinate all but the National Assembly, which has oversight committees for that purpose.

Under the monitoring framework, the vice president, the chairman of the National Planning Commission and the National Economic Council, is at the apex of the hierarchy. However, the Minister of National Planning and deputy chairman of the National Planning Commission had operational command.

The framework scheduled for monitoring of the agenda are:

- Annual report for each year from 2011 to 2013.
- Bi-annual report with effect from 2012 to 2015.
- Quarterly reports with effect from 2012 to 2015.

The Economic Recovery and Growth Plan (2017-2020)

The Economic Recovery and Growth Plan (ERPG) was the medium-term economic development blueprint of the Muhammadu Buhari administration. Its objective was to reverse the Nigerian economy's steady and steep decline at a time the country's economy was in a recession.

The plan built on the strategic implementation plan (SIP) for the 2016 budget of change and aimed to restore economic growth in Nigeria while leveraging the ingenuity and resilience of the Nigerian people.

It is premised on the principle and understanding that the government's role in the 21st century must evolve from that of being an omnibus provider of citizens' needs into a force for eliminating the bottlenecks that impede innovation and market-based solutions.

The plan also recognised the need to leverage science, technology, and innovation and build a knowledge-based economy. It is also consistent with the aspirations of the Sustainable Development Goals (SDGs) given that the initiative addresses its three dimensions of economic, social, and environmental sustainability issues.

The ERPG prides itself as being different from other plans because it put implementation at the core of its delivery strategy. It also claims that, now more than ever before, a strong political determination, commitment, and will exists to push the implementation through.

Its vision was to ensure sustained growth of the Nigerian economy. It is predicated on driving a structural, economic transformation, emphasizing public and private sector efficiency. This aimed to increase national productivity and achieve sustainable diversification of production to significantly grow the economy and achieve maximum welfare for the citizens.

It assigned different implementation plans to MDAs and a delivery unit established in the presidency to drive the overall implementation. The coordination of all efforts and capacity-building for monitoring and implementation would be done by the Ministry of Budget and National Planning.

The plan planned a ramp-up of crude oil production to 2.5 million barrels per day by 2020, the privatisation of selected public enterprises/assets, and revamping local oil refineries to reduce petroleum product imports by 60 percent. It also placed importance on emerging sectors such as the entertainment and creative industries.

The ERPG built on existing sectoral strategies and plans such as the National Industrial Revolution Plan and the Nigeria Integrated Infrastructure Plan. Rather than re-invent the wheel, the ERPG hoped to strengthen the successful components of previous strategies and plans while addressing challenges observed in their implementation.

The plan also envisaged a close partnership between the public and private sectors. It stressed that in implementing the plan, the government would collaborate closely with businesses to deepen their investments in the agriculture, power, manufacturing, solid minerals and service sectors and support the private sector to become the engine of national growth and development.

The ERPG recommended merging the budget and planning functions into one ministry to create a better and stronger link between it and annual budgets. The hope was it would facilitate the plan's preparation process, expedite its implementation, strengthen the macro framework, and ensure budgets are properly aligned with planning, thus promoting effective implementation.

The plan provided for some collaboration and coordination between the federal and state governments for harmony in achieving the same goals as the states have a significant role in its success.

The ERPG was founded on five key principles. They are:

- Focus on tackling constraints of growth
- Leverage the power of the private sector
- Promote national cohesion and social inclusion
- Allow markets to function
- Uphold core values

The broad objectives of the ERPG are restoring growth and investing in Nigerians. It aimed to achieve this through social inclusion, job creation, youth empowerment, and improved human capital.

One significant recurring decimal in the ERGP was the emphasis on implementation. It prioritised macroeconomic stability, envisaging that achieving economic growth depends on a stable microeconomic environment with low inflation, stable exchange rates, and sustainable fiscal and external balances.

Major assumptions of the ERGP are:

It placed much premium on food security as sine qua non for effective plan implementation. In furtherance of this, the plan placed the self-sufficiency target for rice production in 2018 and wheat production by 2019/2020.

The same goes for the energy sector, which was identified as fundamental to nationwide development. As a result, the ERGP planned to increase power generation by delivering at least 10 GW of operational capacity by 2020.

The plan had intentions to accelerate the implementation of the National Industrial Revolution Plan (NIRP) through special economic zones to create 1.5 million jobs by 2020.

For economic growth, real GDP was projected to grow by 4.62 percent on average over the plan's period (2017-2020). The growth is expected to be driven mainly by agriculture and industrial activities, helped by an expected increase in oil prices, non-oil federal receipts, oil production, and resolution of payment arrears, especially joint venture cash calls.

The plan also hoped that increased growth in the non-oil sector, especially agriculture, manufacturing, services, and light industries, will be central to overall GDP growth. In addition, the ERGP contained plans for the government to drive fiscal stimulus through increased spending to stimulate private consumption and investments by businesses. This envisaged dedicating at least 30 percent of the federal budget to capital expenditure.

The Nigeria Vision 2050

On September 10, 2020, Nigeria commenced the process of formulating new long-term and medium-term economic development plans. President Mohammadu Buhari inaugurated a national steering committee

to oversee and actualize a long-term economic development plan—
Nigeria Vision 2050—and a Medium-term National Development Plan
(MTNNDP).

The Nigeria Vision 2050 will be the successor plan to the National
Vision20:2020, while the MTNNDP will succeed the Economic
Recovery and Growth Plan (ERPG) with the main objective to lift 100
million Nigerians out of poverty within ten years.

The national steering committee for the development of these plans
is chaired jointly by Mr Atedo Peterside, a leading private sector player,
and Dr Zainab Ahmed, the Minister of Finance, Budget, and National
Planning. The committee would oversee the governance structure,
comprising the Central Working Group and 26 technical working groups.
It is also expected to oversee the execution of key deliverables, including
recommending measures to ensure continuous implementation of the
plans even after the expiration of the tenure of successive
administrations, including legislation, if required.

The strategies to achieve Vision 2050 include urgently addressing
major constraints to Nigeria's growth and competitiveness, such as
epileptic power supply, and weak infrastructure and institutions, and
aggressively pursuing a structural transformation of the economy from a
mono-product to a diversified and industrialized economy.

Others are to invest in human capital to transform the Nigerian
people into active agents for growth and national development, and to
invest in infrastructure to create an enabling environment for growth,
industrial competitiveness, and sustainable development.

Bibliography

Abasili, C.O.   (2004) Citizens and State Relations: A political Approach. Lagos: Concept publications Limited.

Abdu, H. (2012) In Anakwue, M. (2015) The bourgeoisie and Vision 20:2020 Economic Development Blueprint. A PhD Thesis submitted to the Department of Political Economy and Development Studies, University of Abuja.

Adejumoh, J, Enimola, O and Asabor, I (2019) Will Nigeria win war against abandoned projects?   A report in Daily Independent Newspaper of Sunday December 1, 2019.

Ahmed, M. (2012) In Anakwue, M. (2015) The bourgeoisie and Vision 20:2020 Economic Development Blueprint. A PhD Thesis submitted to the Department of Political Economy and Development Studies, University of Abuja.

Ake, C.(1981), A Political Economy of Africa. Essex: Longman.

Ake, C. (1985) The Political Economy of Nigeria. Lagos: Longman Publishers.

Akinpelu, Y. How federal lawmakers steal billions under the guise of constituency projects- ICPC. A report in Premium Times online Newspaper of December 15, 2019.

Aluko-Olokun, I. "Nigeria's Economy is Still Robust." Tribune Newspaper. Sunday, October 19, 1997.

Anakwue, A. (2019) Politics of Economic Regulation. London: Adonnis & Abbey.

Arndt, H. (1987) Economic Development: The History of An Idea. The University of Chicago Press.

Ayinla, M.A. (1998), Essays on Planning and Budgeting Systems in Nigeria. Ilorin: Berende Publishers.

Ajayi, G. (1999), Internal politics of decolonization and emergence of neo-colonialism in post-independence Nigeria. In G Ajayi (ed): Critical perspectives on Nigeria's socio-political development in 20th century. Lagos: Stebak Books.

Ayinla, M.A. (1998), Essays on Planning and Budgeting Systems in Nigeria. Ilorin: Berende Publishers

Ayo, E.J. (1998), Development Planning in Nigeria. Ibadan: University Press PLC.

Ayobami, A. (2012) About 12,000 federal projects abandoned across Nigeria. A report on Premium Times Newspaper of November 24,

2002.

Backhaus J. (ed) Joseph Alois Schumpeter. The European Heritage in Economics and the Social Sciences, Vol 1, Springer, Boston, MA

Bello, K. (2008) Ideological Bankruptcy in The Political Practice of Nigeria. Keffi: AMD Publishers.

Chapra, U. (1992), Islam and The Economic Challenge. Leicester: The Islamic Foundation.

Chengdan, Q. (2010)Transformation of European States: From Feudalism to Modern. In   Procedia Social and Behavioural Sciences 41 6683-6691. Available online at www.sciencedirect.com.

Dean, E. (1970) Plan Implementation in Nigeria: 1962-1966. Ibadan: Oxford University Press.

Domhoff, W. (1979), The Powers That Be: Processes of Ruling Class Domination in America. New York: Random House.

Dynan, K. (2018) GDP As A Measure of Economic Well-Being. Harvard University Peterson Institute for International Economics. https://www.brookings.edu/research/gdp-as-a-measure-of-economic-well-being/

Fadakinte, M. (2013) The Nature and Character of the Nigerian State: Explaining Election Crisis in a Peripheral State. In the British Journal of Arts and Social Sciences, Vol. 12, No, II.

Fasan, O, (2020) Nigeria: Feudalism Is the Root Cause of the North's Existential Decline. An article in the Vanguard Newspaper of March 12, 2020.

Gboyega, A.   (1989), Nigeria Since Independence: The First Twenty-Five Years, Volume VIII. Public Administration. Ibadan: Heinemann Educational Books.

Goddard, R. et al. (1996),   International Political Economy: State-Marke Relations in the Changing Global Order. Colorado: Lynne Rienner Publishers.

Habineza, J, (2013) In Anakwue, M. (2015) The bourgeoisie and Vision 20:2020

Economic Development Blueprint. A PhD Thesis submitted to the Department of Political Economy and Development Studies, University of Abuja.

Igali, G. (2014) Global Trends in State Formation: An Inquiry into the Origin, Survival and Demise of States. Bloomington, USA: Trafford Publishers.

Igbuzor, O. (2009), Challenges of Development in Nigeria. Lagos: Robito Alliance Publishers.

Ihonvbere, J.O. "The State, Governance and Democratization in Africa: Constraints and Possibilities." Hunger Teachnet, Vol 6. No 3. 1991.

Ijie, B. (2018) Policy Development and Implementation on Nigeria Federal System. A published work sourced from the internet on February 22, 2021.https://www.researchgate.net/publication/328853 757_Policy_Development_and_Implementation_in_Nigeria_Federal _System

Ikeanyibe, M and Imhanlahmi, J. (2009) Local Government Autonomy and Development of Localities in Nigeria: Issues, Problems and Suggestions. In Global journal of social scienes. Vol. 8, No 2, 2009.

Isiekwe, H. (2020) Why the Kaw was designed to favour Tenants at the expense of their Landlords. An Unpublished material sourced from the Internet on September 2, 2020. https://www.academia.edu/1024 4515/WHY_THE_LAW_WAS_DESIGNED_TO_FAVOUR_TE NANTS_AT_THE_EXPENSE_OF_THEIR_LANDLORDS

Iwara, I. (2016) State Capture, Environment and Nigeria's Political Economy. In Journal of Advances In Social Science and Humanities

Kahn, M. (2006) States And Economic Development: What Role? What Risk? An Unpublished work sourced from the internet on September 2, 2020. https://www.odi.org/events/167-states-and-economic-development-what-role-what-risks

Kohli, A. State-Directed Development: Political Power And Industrialization in The Global Periphery: Cambridge University Press, 2012.

Leslie, l. (1960), The great Issues of Politics. New Jersey: Prentice Hall Inc.

Marx, K. (1848), Manifesto of The Communist Party. Beijing: foreign Language Press.

McLellan, D. (1960) Marxism After Marx. V. Lenin Selected Works. Moscow.

Michael, S. _ (2015), The nature and structure of the economy of pre-colonial Nigeria. An internet publication, www.academia.edu/170909 84/the_nature_and_structure_of_the_pre-colonial_Nigeria.

Miliband, R. (1969), The State In Capitalist Society. London: Weidenfeld and Nicolson.

Nasir, J. Lawan: Cost of infrastructure projects in Nigeria highest in the

World. A report on The Cable online Newspaper of July 2, 2019.

Nnoli, O. (ed) (1993) Dead-End to Nigerian Development: An Investigation on The Economic and Political Crisis in Nigeria 1979-1989. Dakar:Codesria.

Nnoli, O. (1986) Introduction To Politics. Enugu: Pan African Centre for Research on Peace and Conflict Resolution.

Obadan, M. (2013) Vision 20:2020 Not Feasible, says Don. A news report on The Nation newspaper of August 14, 2013.

Obikeze, O. Ananti, M. and Onyekwelu, R. (2015) The challenges of ending rural poverty: An appraisal of national poverty eradication programme(NAPEP) In Journal of Policy and Development Studies. Vol. 9, No. 3, May 2015.

Odunlami, L. (1999), Media in Nigeria's Security and Development Vision, Ibadan: Spectrum books limited.

Ogbuagu, C. (1983) The Nigerian Indigenisation Policy: Nationalism or Pragmatism. In African Affairs. Oxford University Press on Behalf of The Royal African Society. Vol. 82, No. 327.

Ogunjimi, S (1997), Public Finance for Polytechnics and ICAN Students. Minna: Leken Productions.

Ojo, G. and Offiong, R (2018)Land Grabbing: Implications of 1978 Land Use Act on Rural Livelihood Sustainability In Cross River State, Nigeria. In International Journal of Development and Economic Sustainability. Vol. 6, No. 5.

Okigbo, P. (1993), Essays in The Public Philosophy of Development The Change And Crisis in The Management of Nigerian Economy. Vol. 2. Enugu: Fourth Dimension Publishing Company Limited.

Okojie, C.(2002), Development Planning In Nigeria Since Independence. In Iyoha, M (ed) Nigerian Economy: Structure, Growth and Development. Benin city:Mindex Publishing.

Okoye, U.C. and Onyeukwu, C. (2007). Sustaining Poverty Reduction Efforts through InterAgency Collaborations in Nigeria In K. Omeje (ed), State, Society relations in Nigeria Democratic Consolidations, Conflicts and reforms. London, Adonnis and Abbey.

Okunbor, K. (2014) Why we built airport, by Lamido. A report on The Nation newspaper, July 22, 2014.

Olafusi, E. (2019) Buhari: N1trn spent on constituency projects in 10 years without impact. A report on The Cable online newspaper. November 19, 2019.

Olaniyi, J. (1998), Foundations of Public Analysis. Ibadan: Sunad Publishers Limited.

Olukoshi, A. (ed) (1993), The politics of Structural Adjustment In Nigeria. Ibadan: Heinemann Education Books Inc.

Oluwajuyitan, J.(2020) Institutionalising Feudalism. An article in the Nation Newspaper, May 7, 2020.

Onoh, J. (1983) The Nigerian Oil Economy. London: Croom Helm.

Onuoha, J. (2008) The State and Economic Reforms in Nigeria: An Explanatory Note on The Capture Theory of Politics. The African Renaissance, Vol 5, Issue 2, Jan, 2008.

Onuoha, J. (1993) What is the State? Enugu: ACENA Publishers.

Osemenan, I. (1987). Project Abandonment: New Watch Magazine, 1: 15.

Oshio, P. (1990) The Indigenous Land Tenure and Nationalization of Land in Nigeria, 10 Boston College Third World Law Journal. Vol. 10, Issue 1, Article 3 http://lawdigitalcommons.bc.edu/twlj/vol10/is s1/3

Poulantzas, N. (1978) State, Power, Socialism. London: Uk Verso

Qayum, A. (1975), Techniques of National Economic Planning. Indiana University Press.

Salawu et all, (2012) Financial Policy and Corporate Performance: An Empirical Analysis of Nigerian Listed Companies. In Journal of economics and finance. Vol. 4, No 4, April 2012.

Schultz, L and Appleby, L. (2019) Investments in Education Support Developing Countries on the Path to Self-Relaince. An article in GPE: Transforming Education as downloaded from the website https://www.globalpartnership.org/blog/investments-health-and-education-support-developing-countries-path-self-reliance.

Schumpeter J. and Backhaus U. (2003) The Theory of Economic Development, In Backhaus J. (ed) Joseph Alois Schumpeter: The European Heritage in Economics and the Social Sciences, Vol 1. Springer, Boston, MA.

See the National Employment Policy, 2017 of the Federal Republic of Nigeria.

See Global Economic Trends 2011. The Challenge of a Job Recovery. An unpublished work by the International Labour Organization.

Seers, D. (1969), The Meaning of Development. Brighton: IDS Communication

Sen, A. (1999) Development as Freedom. New York: Alfred Knopf

Sodipe, A. and Ogunrinnola, I. (2011) Employment and Economic Growth in Nigeria, In International Journal of Business and Social Science, Vol. 2. No 11, June, 2011.

Soludo, C. (2007) Nigeria's Financial System Strategy 2020 Plan. "Our Dream" A presentation as Governor of Central Bank of Nigeria at the International Conference Centre, Abuja.

Tekena, N. Et Al. (1989), Nigeria Since Independence: The First Twenty-Five Years, Volume iv, Ibadan: Heinemann Educational Books.

Todaro, M. And Stephen Smith, C. (2012), Economic Development: Boston, Mass Addison-Wesley.

Umney, C. (2013) The Totalizing MarketIn Marxist Thought. An Unpublixhed working Paper, University of Work and Employment Research Unit (available at website, https://www.academia.edu/3503 325/The_Totalising_Market_in_Marxist_Thought

Usigbe, L. "FG Terminates Lagos-Ibadan Expressway Contract: Julius Berger, RCC to Commence Immediate Reconstruction." The Tribune Newspaper. Tuesday, November 18, 2012.

Uwaleke, U. (2020) Counting the Cost of Nigeria Unrest. An interview conducted on Tuesday October 27, 2020.

Uzoigwe, D. (2007) Economic Development in Nigeria through the Agricultural, Manufacturing and Mining Sectors: An Economic Approach. A thesis submitted to the faculty of Economics and Management Studies, University of Pretoria, South Africa.

Uzor, D. "What Was Wrong With Vision 2010?" The Blueprint, Tuesday, June 5, 2012.

Van Den Berg, A. (1998), The Immanent Utopia: From Marxism on the State to the State of Marxism. New Jersey: Princeton University Press, 1988.

West, D. "Vision 2010 As launching Pad." THIS DAY Newspaper. October 15, 1997.

Williams, S. "Passenger Service Charge: Any Gain From The Bickering? Business Day Newspaper. Thursday, December 15, 2011.

Willyard, K. (2015) Classical Theories of the State and Their Interpretations. In an Academic Blog culled from the internet on July 20, 2020. http://www.katewillyard.com/academic-blog/classical-theories-of-the-state-and-their-reinterpretations

Appendices

Appendix 1. NIGERIA POVERTY AND INEQUALITY REPORT (2019)

States	Poverty Rate (Percentage)
SOKOTO	87.73
TARABA	87.72
JIGAWA	87.02
EBONYI	79.76
ADAMAWA	75.41
ZAMFARA	73.98
YOBE	72.34
NIGER	66.11
GOMBE	62.31
BAUCHI	61.53
ENUGU	58.13
NASARAWA	57.13
KATSINA	56.42
KANO	55.1
PLATEAU	55.1
KEBBI	50.2
KADUNA	43.5
ABUJA (FCT)	38.7
CROSSRIVER	36.3
BENUE	32.9
ABIA	30.7
IMO	28.9
KOGI	28.5
EKITI	28.0
AKWA IBOM	26.8
RIVERS	23.9
BAYELSA	22.6
KWARA	20.4
ANAMBRA	14.8
ONDO	12.5
EDO	12.0
OYO	9.8
OGUN	9.3
OSUN	8.5
DELTA	6.0
LAGOS	4.5
BORNO	0.0 (Not Available)

Source: National Bureau of Statistics

Appendix 2. Universal Basic Education Commission Unaccessed Matching Grant From (2005 - 2019) As Of July 22, 2019

S/N	STATE	2005-2008	2009-2010	2011-2012	2013-2014	2015-2016	2017-2019	TOTAL
1	ABIA	1.38	0.00	26,430,893.96	0.00	0.00	4,477,347,485.7	2,988,805,613.14
2	ADAMAWA	1.38	0.00	0.00	0.00	0.00	2,087,92,9864	2,087,929,865.42
3	AKWA IBOM	1.38	0.00	0.00	0.00	0.00	9,741,857,912.8	705,374,629.15
4	ANAMBRA	1.38	0.00	0.00	0.00	0.00	1,105,374,632.5	1,105,374,633.91
5	BAUCHI	4,866.38	0.00	0.70	0.00	0.00	1,105,369,766.8	1,105,374,633.91
6	BAYELSA	1.38	0.00	0.00	0.00	0.00	1,105,374,632,5	1,105,374,633.91
7	BENUE	1.38	0.00	0.00	0.00	0.00	1,223,465,991.4	1,223,465,992.75
8	BORNO	0.00	0.00	0.00	0.00	0.00	614,097,018.84	614,097,018.84
9	C/ RIVER	1.38	0.00	0.00	0.00	2,027,027.02	614,097,018.84	616,124,047.24
10	DELTA	1.38	0.00	0.00	0.00	0.00	614,097,018.84	614,097,020.22
11	EBONYI	1.38	0.00	0.00	0.00	0.00	614,097,018.84	614,097,020.22
12	EDO	1.38	0.00	0.00	0.00	0.00	1,105,374,632.5	1,105,374,633.91
13	EKITI	1.38	0.00	527,306.70	0.00	1,102,670,626.38	2,210,749,265	4,477,470,982.05
14	ENUGU	2.38	0.00	0.00	0.00	90,600,548.29	2,391,717,816.1	3,464,873,598.26
15	GOMBE	1.38	0.00	0.00	0.00	0.00	614,097,018.84	614,097,020.22
16	IMO	1.38	0.00	0.00	0.00	0.00	614,097,018.84	614,097,020.22
17	JIGAWA	1.38	0.00	-0.04	0.00	0.00	1,351,013,441.4	1,351,013,442.78
18	KADUNA	1.38	0.00	-0.04	0.00	0.00	614,097,018.84	614,097,020.18
19	KANO	1.38	0.00	0.00	0.00	0.00	614,097,018.84	614,097,020.22
20	KATSINA	1.38	0.00	0.00	0.00	0.00	614,097,018.84	614,097,020.22
21	KEBBI	1.38	0.00	0.00	0.00	0.00	614,097,018.84	614,097,020.22
22	KOGI	1.38	0.00	0.00	0.00	0.00	614,097,018.84	614,097,020.22
23	KWARA	1.38	0.00	1,000.00	952,297,297.30	1,918,783,783.78	3,374,273,047.5	6,245,355,130.05
24	LAGOS	1.38	0.00	0.00	0.00	0.00	614,097,018.84	614,097,020.22
25	NASARAWA	1.38	0.00	1,000.00	0.00	434,177,926.54	3,374,273,047.5	3,808,451,975.51
26	NIGER	1.38	0.00	5,000,000.00	0.00	0.00	1,100,374,632.5	1,105,374,633.91
27	OGUN	1.38	0.00	0.00	0.00	0.00	1,105,374,632.5	1,105,374,633.91
28	ONDO	1.38	0.00	0.00	0.00	0.00	614,097,018.84	614,097,020.22
29	OSUN	1.38	0.00	0.00	0.00	0.00	2,087,929,864	2,087,929,865.42
30	OYO	1.38	0.00	0.00	0.00	0.00	2,087,929,864	2,087,929,865.42
31	PLATEAU	1.38	0.00	0.00	0.00	0.00	2,290,877,911.5	2,290,877,912.89
32	RIVERS	1.38	0.00	0.00	0.00	0.00	614,097,018.84	614,097,020.22
33	SOKOTO	1.38	0.00	0.00	0.00	0.00	614,097,018.84	614,097,020.22
34	TARABA	1.38	0.00	0.00	0.00	0.00	614,097,018.84	614,097,020.22
35	YOBE	1.38	0.00	0.00	0.00	0.00	614,097,018.84	614,097,020.22
36	ZAMFARA	1.38	0.00	0.00	0.00	0.00	1,105,374,632.5	1,105,374,633.91
37	F.C.T. ABUJA	1.37	0.68	0.00	0.00	0.26	614,097,018.84	614,097,021.15
	CURRICULUM	0.00	0.00	0.00	0.00	0.00	0.00	0.00
	GRAND TOTAL	**4,915.67**	**0.68**	**31,960,201.28**	**952,297,297.30**	**3,548,259,912.27**	**47,080,352,373.1**	**51,612,874,700.70**

Appendix 3. Capital Projects Envisaged for the Third National Development Plan

Sector	Total All Governments (2)	Federal Government	Total All State	Anambra	Bauchi	Bendel	Benue	Borno	Cross River
Agriculture	1,681.273	765.028	916.245	11.088	31.019	67.699	45.985	18.640	76.603
Irrigation	638.951	535.086	103.865	....	5.630	___	___	4.820	___
Livestock	486.829	284.018	202.811	8.502	7.113	___	13.944	7.305	9.396
Forestry	135.644	36.130	99.154	3.600	2.605	18.100	4.245	3.104	15.970
Fishery	100.32	54.560	45.472	0.600	0.155	1.550	1.790	0.979	6.300
Manufacturing and craft	5,485.877	5,055.468	430.409	27.754	10.892	54.007	27.134	13.000	46.034
Mining and quarrying	2,645.924	___	___	___		___	___	___	___
Commerce and finance	775.984	498.930	277.524	12.760		10.500	11.675	7.000	36.819
Co-operative and supply	208.688	12.200	96.488	4.040	4.950	11.412	4.085	7.092	10.355
Power	1,285.325	1,056.825	228.500	10.000	10.000	25.000	12.000	10.000	12.000
Transport	9,677.541	8,064.571	1,612.970	124.740	49.533	200.193	56.141	48.540	136.489
Communications	3,529.195	3,529.195	___	___	___	___	___	___	___
Sub-total	26,651.733	22,637.935	4,013.798	203.084	130.017	385.017	176.999	120.480	349.966

Social Service

Education	3,222.069	1,894.314	1,327.755	92.236	78.018	68.850	49.330	7.092	87.967
Health	1,172.931	992.660	480.271	35.500	42.500	38.659	21.850	16.750	27.350
Information	387.183	252.850	134.333	7.800	2.722	6.889	5.995	7.013	20.650
Labour	27.413	27.413	___	___	___	___	___	___	___
Social development and sports	202.172	46.530	155.642	6.299	8.957	6.661	10.077	6.978	8.750
Sub-total	5,011.768	2,913.767	2,098.001	145.835	116.063	130.227	80.081	120.480	144.717

Regional Development

Water supply	1,549.023	500.000	1,049.023	84.000	22.224	101.400	44.580	40.610	41.600
Sewerage, drainage and refuse disposal	462.247	154.500	307.747	15.715	1.550	57.9604.470	4.470	7.500	7.100
Housing	2,256.390	2,000.650	255.740	9.500	3.500	45.000	5.000	5.000	15.000
Town and country planning	1,589.295	744.163	845.132	48.325	13.500	33.360	15.000	25.490	51.400
Community development	177.046	___	177.046	5.500	7.034	11.600	5.700	5.100	7.400
SUB TOTAL	6,034.001	3,339.313	2,634.688	163.040	47.808	249.320	74.750	83.700	122.500

Defence and security	4,350.249	4,350.249	___	___	___	___	___	___	___
General administration	1,266.258	619.833	646.425	24.981	40.286	40.817	39.243	24.978	46.200
Sub-total	5,616.507	4,970.082	646.425	24.981	40.286	40.817	39.243	24.978	46.200
Grand total	43,314.009	33,921.097	9,392.912	536.940325	334.184	806.024	397.764	309.239	6

ation	8.895	------	---------	57.900	____	____	17.075	____	___	___	___	___	9.545
stock	11.873	7.205	12.560	23.664	7.321	15.928	6.990	6.715	9.295	14.900	9.537	7.400	14.441
estry	6.060	1.319	6.065	5.610	8.887	0.500	2.355	3.528	8.891	3.990	6.688	2.000	7.520
ery	0.755	0.842	0.119	1.560	1.269	17.650	0.435	3.620	0.950	2.450	1.610	2.038	0.800
hufacturing craft	12.930	29.950	17.248	18.864	27.782	32.246	7.200	10.550	13.620	21.400	17.770	32.928	9.100
ing and rrying	----		----	----	----	-	-	-	----	-			
nmerce and nce	7.300	14.550	20.804	18.385	24.014	18.000	7.065	5.400	6.300	3.500	12.226	41.100	12.026
perative and ply	4.000	4.232	5.800	4.250	7.460	1.750	2.430	1.748	2.634	5.930	0.751	9.000	3.723
ver	10.000	10.000	10.000	12.000	12.000	6.000	10.000	12.000	15.000	14.500	15.000	8.000	15.000
nsport	57.439	90.278	78.123	89.697	97.055	46.585	54.195	88.189	99.385	93.245	73.976	56.130	73.017
nmunications	----	----	----	----	----	----	----	----	----	----	----	----	----
-total	15.454	220.845		234.978	300.128	244.284	154.983	127.863	175.019	222.120	235.588	167.360	214.046	198.089

ucation	82.703	55.606	124.129	140.970	74.788	35.642	39.799	24.428	31.956	47.860	68.804	80.300	78.485
alth	24.650	40.147	19.658	27.156	15.000	40.848	20.915	12.545	15.962	15.590	16.151	27.855	21.185
formation	3.150	9.275	3.191	4.850	8.940	3.300	2.685	6.343	4.379	13.924	9.189	10.310	3.718
bour	----	----	----	----	----	----	----	----	----	----	----	----	
cial velopment d sports	9.221	7.050	4.925	8.492	17.260	15.860	6.240	4.307	5.789	6.370	4.830	9.350	8.226
b-total	119.724	112.078	151.903	181.468	115.988	95.650	69.639	47.623	58.086	83.744	98.974	127.815	111.614

Education	3,222.069	1,894.314	1,327.755	92.236	78.018	68.850	49.330	7.092	87.967
Health	1,172.931	992.660	480.271	35.500	42.500	38.659	21.850	16.750	27.350
Information	387.183	252.850	134.333	7.800	2.722	6.889	5.995	7.013	20.650
Labour	27.413	27.413	___	___	___	___	___	___	___
Social development and sports	202.172	46.530	155.642	6.299	8.957	6.661	10.077	6.978	8.750
Sub-total	5,011.768	2,913.767	2,098.001	145.835	116.063	130.227	80.081	120.480	144.717

Water Supply	13.310	58.380	88.269	59.500	60.500	46.400	46.580	45.020	71.250	101.920	42.520	18.800	62.160
Sewage, Drainage and refuse disposal	1.980	5.320	13.150	14.490	4,180	70.000	6.840	9.000	4.400	43.700	4.870	26.500	9.000
Housing	3.500	15.000	13.300	23.860	3.500	16.000	15.000	10.000	10.000	10.000	10.000	10.000	32.580
Town and country planning	17.050	106.159	23.590	36.041	45.857	125.570	21.960	29.650	66.793	70.320	16.727	53.550	44.790
Community development	7.870	6.400	12.707	17.707	16.000	39.090	8.395	4.100	1.500	___	5.123	1.200	15.890
Sub-total	43.710	191.259	150.379	150.961	130.037	297.064	98.775	97.770	153.943	225.940	79.262	110.050	164.420

Defence and security	___	___	—	—	—	—	—	—	___	___	___	___	___
General administration	32.097	44.100	34.450	57.162	28.924	30.610	38.298	25.326	35.950	13.367	22.051	39.127	28.448
Sub-total	322.097	44.100	34.450	57.162	28.924	30.610	38.298	25.326	35.950	13.367	22.051	39.127	28.448
Grand Total	346.985	567.037	572.638	689.719	519.233	578.307	334.575.	345.738	470.099	558.639	367.647	491.038	502.571